Mysterious Polynesia: The Myths, Legends, and Mysteries of th

By Charles River Editors

Erin A. Kirk-Cuomo's picture of Maori warriors performing a dance

About Charles River Editors

Charles River Editors is a boutique digital publishing company, specializing in bringing history back to life with educational and engaging books on a wide range of topics. Keep up to date with our new and free offerings with this 5 second sign up on our weekly mailing list, and visit Our Kindle Author Page to see other recently published Kindle titles.

We make these books for you and always want to know our readers' opinions, so we encourage you to leave reviews and look forward to publishing new and exciting titles each week.

Introduction

Moai at Rano Raraku, Easter Island

By the mid-17th century, the existence of a land in the south referred to as Terra Australis was generally known and understood by the Europeans, and incrementally, its shores were observed and mapped. Van Diemen's Land, an island off the south coast of Australia now called Tasmania, was identified in 1642 by Dutch mariner Abel Tasman, and a few months later, the intrepid Dutchman would add New Zealand to the map of the known world.

In 1769, Captain James Cook's historic expedition in the region would lead to an English claim on Australia, but before he reached Australia, he sailed near New Zealand and spent weeks mapping part of New Zealand's coast. Thus, he was also one of the first to observe and take note of the indigenous peoples of the two islands. His instructions from the Admiralty were to endeavor at all costs to cultivate friendly relations with tribes and peoples he might encounter, and to regard any native people as the natural and legal possessors of any land they were found to occupy. Cook, of course, was not engaged on an expedition of colonization, so when he encountered for the first time a war party of Māori, he certainly had no intention of challenging their overlordship of *Aotearoa*, although he certainly was interested in discovering more about them.

It was on October 6, 1769 that land was sighted from the masthead of the HMS *Endeavour*. The ostensible purpose of the expedition was to observe the transit of Venus across the Sun, but in sealed orders, to be opened only when these astrological observations were complete, he was instructed to search for evidence of the fabled *Terra Australis*. Approaching from the east, having rounded Cape Horn and calling in at Tahiti, the *Endeavour* arrived off the coast of New Zealand, and two days later it dropped anchor in what would later be known as Poverty Bay. No sign of life or habitation was seen until on the morning of the 9 October when smoke was observed to be rising inland, indicating that the territory was indeed inhabited. Cook and a group of sailors set off for shore in two boats and leaving four men behind to mind the boats, the remainder set off inland over a line of low hills. The sentries, however, were surprised by the arrival of a group of four Māori, who adopted an aggressive posture, and when one lifted a lance to hurl, he was immediately shot down.

Cook and his landing party hurried back, and after a few rounds were fired, the Māori retreated, and the party returned to the *Endeavour*. The next morning, however, another landing was made, and while some cautious communication was made possible by the fact that Cook had on his staff a Polynesian by the name of Tupaia, whose language was similar, the encounter was no less hostile. When, once again, an aggressive move was made by a Māori, a jittery sailor fired, and another Māori was killed. This was the preliminary to a more aggressive encounter yet, as the Māori attempted to board and kidnap a ship's boy, presumably with a view to eating him. A volley of shots was fired, however, and yet more Māori killed, after which Cook and his crew left the scene and continued their observations offshore.

Cook undertook two voyages to the region of the South Pacific, during which time the "Polynesian" triangle – Hawaii, Easter Island and New Zealand – was brought into the scope of European knowledge, so he and the scientists on board were able to claim at least some superficial appreciation of the Polynesian race. There was no doubt that the Māori, although heirs to a uniquely evolved society, represented a derivative of wider Polynesian society although how and when they made the vast crossing to New Zealand could hardly be guessed at.

Taking into account similarities of appearance, customs and languages spread across a vast region of scattered islands, it was obvious that the Polynesian race emerged from a single origin, and that origin Cook speculated was somewhere in the Malay Peninsula or the "East Indies." In this regard, he was not too far from the truth. The origins of the Polynesian race have been fiercely debated since then, and it was only relatively recently, through genetic and linguistic research, that it can now be stated with certainty that the Polynesian race originated on the Chinese mainland and the islands of Taiwan, the Philippines, Malaysia and Indonesia. Oceania was, indeed, the last major region of the Earth to be penetrated and settled by people, and Polynesia was the last region of Oceania to be inhabited. The vehicle of this expansion was the outrigger canoe, and aided by tides and wind patterns, a migration along the Malay Archipelago, and across the wide expanses of the South Pacific, began sometime between 3000 and 1000 BCE, reaching the western Polynesian Islands in about 900 BCE.

The name Polynesia derives from the ancient Greek meaning "many islands." The word was first used to describe the entirety of the South Sea Islands by the 18th century French writer and traveler Charles de Brosses, but technically, Polynesia refers specifically to an area described by a vast triangle that stretches across the southern Pacific, with Hawaii, Easter Island and New Zealand serving as the points. Close to the center of this triangle lies Tahiti, with the west limit defined by Samoa and Tonga, with a slight irregularity in the western edge of the triangle that serves to exclude Fiji, the Solomon Islands, the New Hebrides, and a handful of Melanesian and Micronesian islands. The Melanesian demographic tends to differ quite dramatically from the Polynesian in both appearance and culture, the former tending to be of darker complexion, while the latter is more characteristic of the South Seas islanders of popular mythology.

Furthermore, not all of the islands included in the broad delineation of Polynesia are the tiny islets and atolls of popular imagination, resplendent with blue lagoons, white sand beaches and pristine coral reefs. Most are located within the tropics and have all the characteristics of an island paradise, but many others, such as Easter Island, the Chatham Islands, and New Zealand, lie well to the south and are, as a consequence, temperate in climate and biology.

While the timing of the populations' movements can be accurately plotted, the motivations and methodology have tended to come to light only through the study of the oral tradition and the folklore associated with many dispersed, but culturally associated peoples. Indeed, when scholars go through the traditions and mythology passed down by people who are dispersed across thousands of miles of water and islands, they are amazed at the striking similarities. Typically, the cultural memories related to these waves of migration speak of warfare and internecine quarrels, often with the defeated chief or king leading an expedition away and thereafter assuming the role of the "first man" in the creation of a new society and political structure.

Mysterious Polynesia: The Myths, Legends, and Mysteries of the Polynesians chronicles some of these remarkable stories, as well as lingering mysteries across the region. Along with pictures of important people, places, and events, you will learn about Polynesia like never before.

Mysterious Polynesia: The Myths, Legends, and Mysteries of the Polynesians

About Charles River Editors

Introduction

    The Settlement of Polynesia

    A Common System

    Creation and Origin

    Heroes and Tricksters

    Moai

    Mythology and Conspiracy Theories on Easter Island

    Online Resources

    Bibliography

Free Books by Charles River Editors

Discounted Books by Charles River Editors

The Settlement of Polynesia

"I have always found them of a brave, noble, open and benevolent disposition, but they are a people that will never put up with an insult if they have an opportunity to resent it." – Captain James Cook

On December 13, 1642, a Dutch survey expedition led by Abel Tasman and comprised of two ships, *Heemskerck* and *Zeehaen*, encountered in the South Pacific what Tasman later described as "a large land uplifted high." What Tasman was in fact looking at was the South Island of New Zealand, and the uplifted high land consisted of the Southern Alps. This land Tasman declared "*Staten Landt,*" or "State Land," and a few days later the small flotilla drifted into Cook Strait.[1] There the two ships anchored in a natural harbor now known as "*Mohua,*" or as it is known today, Golden Bay. There Tasman found a deeply indented shoreline and calm waters, fringed by wooded hills, and gifted with a mild and temperate climate. It certainly was a pleasing sight, and Tasman earmarked it as a country perfectly suited to future European settlement.

A contemporary portrait believed to depict Tasman and his family

---

[1] There are different versions of this naming. Another is that Tasman believed it to be connected to Argentina's Staten Island, or *Isla de los Estados*.

Then, quite unexpectedly, this utopian aspect was shattered when a flotilla of war canoes detached itself from shore and rushed out to meet them. A brief skirmish followed, and a few Dutch sailors were killed before a round of shots was fired that immediately dispersed the attackers. The sides separated and the natives returned to shore. They had never encountered ballistics before, so the experience undoubtedly scared them, but Tasman quickly hoisted sail and hurried back to open water. He later wrote of the encounter, "In the evening about one hour after sunset we saw many lights on land and four vessels near the shore, two of which betook themselves towards us. When our two boats returned to the ships reporting that they had found not less than thirteen fathoms of water, and with the sinking of the sun (which sank behind the high land) they had been still about half a mile from the shore. After our people had been on board about one glass, people in the two canoes began to call out to us in gruff, hollow voices. We could not in the least understand any of it; however, when they called out again several times we called back to them as a token answer. But they did not come nearer than a stone's shot. They also blew many times on an instrument, which produced a sound like the moors' trumpets. We had one of our sailors (who could play somewhat on the trumpet) play some tunes to them in answer."

Tasman named the place Murderer's Bay and continued on, arriving next in the Tongan Archipelago. To the Dutch captain, who had already touched the shores of *Terra Australis*, or "New Holland" as he left it, this first encounter with the natives of New Zealand was sobering. The Australian Aboriginals he had previously met were either friendly or semi-wild, fleeing to the bush like hares at the first sight of a white man. He had certainly never expected to be met on shore by a war party, and he immediately understood that anyone attempting to conquer and settle this land would certainly need to be prepared to fight for it.

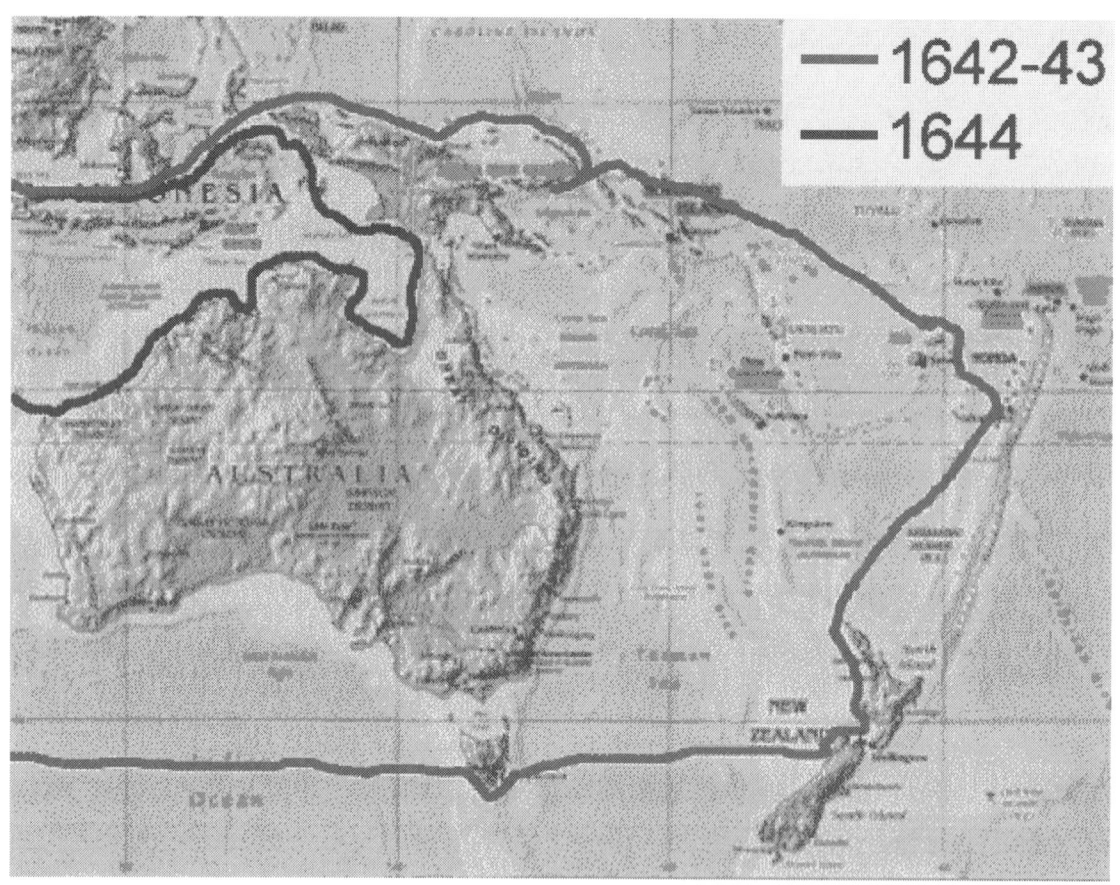

A map of Tasman's voyages in the region

A contemporary depiction of Murderer's Bay

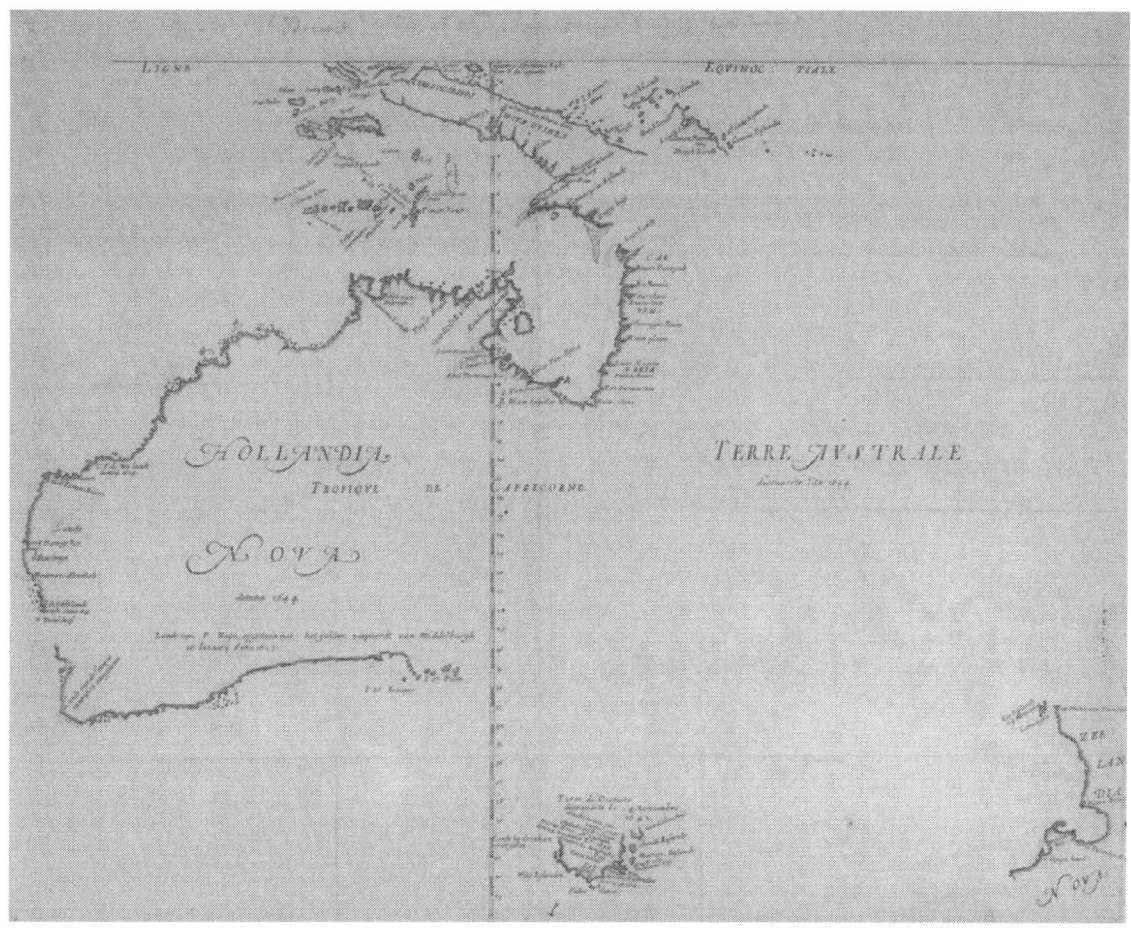

A 1645 map of the region

Archeologists have since explained this initial encounter as the unexpected arrival of an entirely unknown race into an area of settlement and agriculture, and the natural impulse that the indigenous people would feel to protect it. Nonetheless, this first European encounter with the Māori must certainly have presented a striking and intimidating picture. Warlike and tribal, the Māori were then, as they are now, flamboyant and decorative, fond of rituals and ceremonies, and accustomed to warfare as a cultural expression and means of inhabiting an accommodating land. Their distinctive tattoos, both erotic and totemic, were unique and striking expressions of a robust and violent, but also deeply accomplished society.

A 19th century depiction of Māoris

Abel Tasman has long been considered the first European to make contact with New Zealand and its people, but new scholarship has theorized that the first European encounter with New Zealand took place over a century earlier by the Portuguese. It was in the year 1498 that the first Portuguese flotilla arrived on the coast of India, seeding Portuguese settlements along the coasts of India and East Africa. It has since been discovered that a great many of the fundamental achievements in exploration attributed to British, and other European explorers, were in fact preceded by Portuguese travelers and explorers. In this instance, the basis of the theory is simply that Portuguese exploradores were simple and illiterate men, and many of their early feats of exploration were never recorded. It is also true that they explored the trade in slaves, and thus they courted anonymity. Quite often, Portuguese travelers and commercial explorers were simply Portuguese speaking natives or half-castes, and their work also tended to be disregarded.

The notion, therefore, of Portuguese ships making first landfall in Australia and New Zealand is not entirely outlandish. Upon rounding the southern tip of the Indian subcontinent, and crossing the Bay of Bengal, the Malay Archipelago forms a natural conduit in the direction of Australia. The Portuguese founded numerous settlements in these regions, most notably Timor, located just a few hundred miles across the Sea of Timor to the coast of Western Australia. There is also strong material evidence that the Portuguese were aware of the existence of *Terra Australis*, in particular in reference to the "Dieppe Maps," a series of sixteenth century French world maps that portray the "Java la Grande" as corresponding to the northwest coast of

Australia and scattered with Gallicized Portuguese place names. Artifacts thought to be of Portuguese origin have also been unearthed in adjacent coastal regions, and so the theory of prior Portuguese discovery of Australia, if not New Zealand, carries water. It is certainly not a great leap of imagination then to suppose that Portuguese ships, having come this far, might cross the Tasman Sea and set eyes on New Zealand.

Curiously, evidence of very early Spanish visits to New Zealand is a little bit stronger. In the northern Spanish city of La Coruna, a "pohutukawa" tree, native only to New Zealand, can be found. This specimen is estimated to be between 400 and 500 years old, and it is hard to imagine how a tree like that reached the Spanish coast unless a Spanish ship had collected it.

Either way, the first map to feature the name *Nova Zeelandia* was published by the Dutch in 1645, and no substantive European effort was made to exploit or visit this territory until at least a century later. After Abel Tasman, the next recorded European visit would be that of Captain James Cook.

In 1767, the Royal Society persuaded King George III to allocate funds for it to send an astronomer to the Pacific, and on January 1, 1768, the London Annual Register reported, "Mr. Banks, Dr. Solander, and Mr. Green the astronomer, set out for Deal, to embark on board the Endeavour, Captain Cook, for the South Seas, under the direction of the royal society, to observe the transit of Venus next summer, and to make discoveries." Mr. Banks was Joseph Banks, a botanist, and he brought along Dr. Daniel Solander, a Swedish naturalist. Charles Green was at that time the assistant to Nevil Maskelyne, the Astronomer Royal. The expedition, which would leave later in 1768, would be captained by Cook, a war veteran who had recently fought in the French & Indian War against the French in North America.

King George III

Banks

Solander

What the article did not mention was that the Admiralty was also hoping to find the famed Terra Australis Incognita, the legendary "unknown southern land." This came out later, when the *London Gazetteer* reported on August 18, 1768, "The gentlemen, who are to sail in a few days for George's Land, the new discovered island in the Pacific ocean, with an intention to observe the Transit of Venus, are likewise, we are credibly informed, to attempt some new discoveries in that vast unknown tract, above the latitude 40."

When Cook's expedition began in 1768, it included more than 80 men, consisting of 73 sailors and 12 members of the Royal Marines. Presumably, the expedition was supposed to be for entirely scientific – and hence peaceful – purposes. The *Endeavour* left Plymouth on August 26, 1768, and Cook landed at Matavai Bay, Tahiti, on April 13, 1769. The most important task at hand, other than day-to-day survival, was preparing to observe the transit of Venus that would occur on June 3.

Having completed the scientific assignments, the *Endeavour* next set sail in search of Terra Australis. After sailing for nearly two months, the crew earned the prize of being only the second group of Europeans to ever visit New Zealand. They arrived on October 6, 1769, and Cook described a harrowing experience when the men came ashore: "MONDAY, 9th October. …I went ashore with a Party of men in the Pinnace and yawl accompanied by Mr. Banks and Dr. Solander. We landed abreast of the Ship and on the East side of the River just mentioned; but seeing some of the Natives on the other side of the River of whom I was desirous of speaking with, and finding that we could not ford the River, I order'd the yawl in to carry us over, and the pinnace to lay at the Entrance. In the mean time the Indians made off. However we went as far as their Hutts which lay about 2 or 300 Yards from the water side, leaving 4 boys to take care of the Yawl, which we had no sooner left than 4 Men came out of the woods on the other side the River, and would certainly have cut her off had not the People in the Pinnace discover'd them and called to her to drop down the Stream, which they did, being closely persued by the Indians. The coxswain of the Pinnace, who had the charge of the Boats, seeing this, fir'd 2 Musquets over their Heads; the first made them stop and Look round them, but the 2nd they took no notice of; upon which a third was fir'd and kill'd one of them upon the Spot just as he was going to dart his spear at the Boat. At this the other 3 stood motionless for a Minute or two, seemingly quite surprised; wondering, no doubt, what it was that had thus kill'd their Comrade; but as soon as they recovered themselves they made off, dragging the Dead body a little way and then left it. Upon our hearing the report of the Musquets we immediately repair'd to the Boats, and after viewing the Dead body we return'd on board."

Over the following weeks, Cook devoted himself to making a detailed map of the New Zealand coast. Sailing west, Cook hoped to reach Van Diemen's Land, known today as Tasmania, but instead, the winds forced him north, leading him and his men to the southeastern coast of Australia.

Cook

A replica of Cook's ship, *Endeavour*

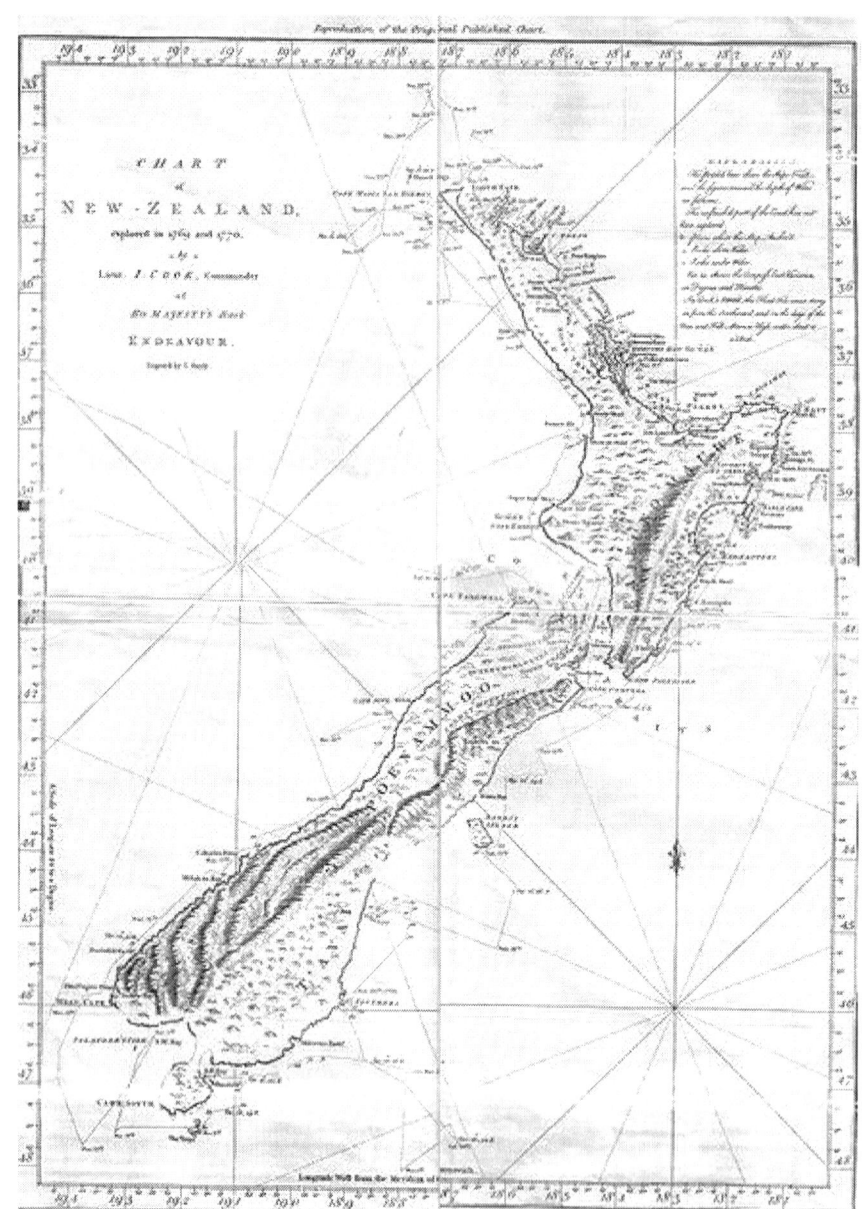

Cook's map of New Zealand's shore

Thus, it was Cook who would Anglicize the name to New Zealand, and on both of his subsequent voyages, Cook returned to New Zealand, but only to cruise the coast and touch lightly on the shore.

Cook's expedition may have been for the purposes of science on the surface, but when he claimed the new territory, the British realized it might serve as a center of future British maritime power and trade in the region. Indeed, as it turned out, that region that would soon be of significant interest to the British because of the American Revolution.

The American colonists, although patriotic and committed, could never have taken on the

British Empire unassisted. A vast anti-British coalition formed in Europe, which provided the political, economic and material bulwark of the Revolution. Russia's Catherine the Great was the prime mover in what came to be known as the League of Armed Neutrality, which facilitated the free flow of money and materiel to North America, provided as aid and assistance by the non-belligerent powers. These, although hardly non-belligerent, included France, which was almost never unwilling to oppose the English, as well as Prussia, the Holy Roman Empire, the Netherlands, Portugal, Spain, and Ottoman Turkey.

After the 1783 Treaty of Paris, the British and the new United States somewhat reconciled, while the French, Dutch, and Spanish continued their bitterly anti-English campaign. In combination, they outstripped British maritime power, and they were in a position to challenge British trade with India and China, the cornerstone of the colossal wealth machine that was British East Indian trade.

At the time, the broad pattern of British trade saw British ships embarking south from England, sailing with the currents across the Atlantic, before striking east via the Cape of Good Hope to India. They would then load up on opium grown under duress by the Indians and ship it to China, where it was sold under duress to the Chinese. For the return journey, tea and various other exotic produce from India were acquired.

Vital to this trade equation was the Cape of Good Hope, a Dutch possession since 1652, and a pivotal strategic maritime position. As far as the British were concerned, the Cape of Good Hope was, at least for the time being, the weak link in the chain. The Dutch were allied with the French, and in addition to the Cape of Good Hope, the Dutch also held the important Ceylonese port of Trincomalee, from which they and their French allies were in a position to threaten British India and British trade interests throughout the region.

If push came to shove and the Cape of Good Hope became unavailable, the British trading fleet would be forced to utilize the east coast of South America, dealing with numerous Spanish and Spanish allied regimes inimical to the British, after which the Cape Horn or Magellan Straits would require negotiation before the long haul across the South Pacific to India. This would certainly not have been ideal.

Then there was the more subtle question of basic raw materials. The Royal Navy, the largest single maritime force in existence, had stripped the British Isles of timber reserves to the extent that a fleet of wooden ships could not be domestically sustained. British timber supplies that supported the local ship-building industries not only came mainly from Russia, but also other Baltic nations. However, in the aftermath of the American Revolution, Russia had become rather estranged and could no longer entirely be trusted. An average Royal Navy or merchant ship of the line utilized more than one mast, which was often several hundred feet tall, and these frequently required repair and replacement. So did the sails and the ships themselves. Denmark and Sweden, alternative sources of timber for the British, were also now of uncertain status, having signed on with the Russian sponsored pro-American League of Armed Neutrality.

It certainly was a hostile world for the British in the late 18th century, even as the British stood to benefit most from international trade. The Royal Navy and the British maritime fleet dominated the major maritime trade routes, but they did so from a position with almost no friends, and ultimately, if Britain could not rely on the cooperation of any other European powers, then the alternative was simply to make do alone. Cook happened to be of the opinion that the only major sources of timber and flax in the Pacific region were to be found in New Zealand and Norfolk Island, located some 1,000 miles northeast of Botany Bay. Nonetheless, it was his opinion that Botany Bay represented the most viable location for a permanent British colony.

Meanwhile, the anti-British alliance continued to ferment in the aftermath of the French Revolution. The French were deeply embittered by their ejection from North America, and for that matter, so were the British, but there was little to be gained by either side crying over spilled milk. However, the French remained deeply interested in India, which was still not comprehensively dominated by the British, and thus still vulnerable to a robust French effort at a takeover. In fact, the French were negotiating a treaty with Ottoman Egypt that would allow French use of Egyptian soil in general communication with her surviving outposts in India. Those outposts were fortified with apparently decommissioned gunships, and a military alliance was formalized with the Dutch for the use of port facilities at the Cape of Good Hope and other Dutch bases in the Pacific.

As a result, in the wake of Cook's voyages, a robust body of commercial explorers, consisting of European whaling fleets, began to probe the New Zealand shoreline for whales and fur seals. It was they who founded the first settlements, and they would be the first to make substantive contact with the Māoris.

When and under what circumstances the first Polynesians arrived on the shores of New Zealand remains a source of acrimonious debate, and in the last century, the Māori's claim to first-nation status has been somewhat complicated by the possibility that an earlier, less developed population known as the Moriori populated the island of New Zealand long before the Māori and were driven to extinction by the more developed and aggressive Māori. Others claim that the Moriori were simply a branch of Māori.

A political overtone to much of this debate is inescapable. With no written language, the history of the Māori has been recorded and has tended to survive through oral tradition. Admirers and collectors of oral tradition frequently swear that oral sources are usually unimpeachable, and perhaps that is so, but the date and circumstances of the Māori's arrival nonetheless remain vague and incomplete.

A common misfortune of societies without a written language is that their history tends to be written by their enemies, and certainly the early leaders in Māori ethnography and chroniclers of Māori history were European. Among these was a renowned English ethnologist by the name of Percy Smith, who was only 10 years old when his family emigrated from England. Smith led the first efforts to gather and record Māori oral tradition, and through this process, he arrived at 750 CE as the most likely date of the first Polynesian contact with New Zealand. That said, he further postulated that the first substantial Polynesian settlement of the islands occurred about six centuries later, with the arrival of the "Great Fleet."

Smith

The Great Fleet was Percy Smith's pet theory, backed up by various versions of the story relayed to him through his research, but never categorically proven. Thus, it remains a theory to this day. In essence, the Great Fleet was believed to be a large and organized migration, embarking from somewhere in the region of the Cook and Society Islands, that arrived on the shores of New Zealand as an organized colonizing party. It may have been the first of many similar waves.

This version of the story asserts that around 750 BCE, a Polynesian explorer and adventurer by the name of Kupe arrived on the shores of an uninhabited land, leaving soon afterwards never to return. Three centuries later, Toi and Whātonga, also Polynesian explorers, arrived, and this time a primitive and nomadic race, the Moriori, had taken up residence. Presumably, the intelligence accumulated on both of these voyages was retained, for in 1350, a fleet of seven voyaging canoes (waka) arrived on North Island, originating from the region of Tahiti. These people, to be known by themselves as Māori, or the "ordinary ones," were a comparatively advanced, warlike and agricultural people, and before long they wiped out the Moriori and expanded to take over both islands.

Percy Smith established the basics of this idea, and thereafter it was generally accepted by both the Māori and Europeans. In fact, it remained the acknowledged version at least until the 1970s. Currently, the date of the first arrivals is set at 1280 CE, arriving from east Polynesia with a founding population numbering in the hundreds. Beyond that, not much can be added to the First Fleet theory, and as such, with one or two variations, it remains the most plausible.

Whenever the Māori arrived, they found a lush and forested land, with no particular extremes of climate or landscape, and with abundant wildlife. The latter included several now-extinct species of moa, a large and flightless bird weighing up to 500 pounds. Without natural land predators, the Moa were easy to hunt and became the first reliable food source. The bird is credited largely with providing a survival bridge between colonization and the establishment of viable agriculture. The moa was hunted to extinction, dying out sometime between 1300 and 1400.

The colder and more unpredictable climate of South Island created a somewhat greater dependence on hunting than agriculture, so the moa was hunted not only for food but also for its hide. From this, and the hide of the ubiquitous kiwi, came the unique feathered cloaks of the Māori. Seals were also commonly hunted, and foraging for shellfish and estuary fishing augmented a diet largely comprising yams and sweet potatoes.

A museum restoration of a moa

The sweet potato, the kūmara, was the main crop brought across with the early Polynesian settlers, and it proved viable under these new conditions. The Māori were generally skilled in producing agricultural implements, adzes and hoes, using stone and abundant hardwood, and it was not long before agricultural settlements were founded. The kūmara then became the basis of the Māori diet, in particular on North Island, where they grew well. It could be stored for long periods and eaten in combination with fish or other flesh. Other food crops were the taro, a starchy root crop, various yams, and the paper mulberry, which was used to make a type of bark cloth.

When the moa was eventually driven to extinction, Māori society was sufficiently established that alternatives were available. The kūmara remained the most important dietary staple, supplemented by fish and shellfish, and fishing became so central to the Māori domestic economy that strict conventions, or tapu, evolved in regards to who could fish where, when they could fish, and under what circumstances. These conventions still create tensions today.

While New Zealand's climate was for the most part nice, it was a great deal less benign than the islands from which they had come, and a more substantial style of domestic architecture was required. George French Angas, an English naturalist, explorer, and artist, was one of the earliest visual recorders of day-to-day Māori life, and he was eventually appointed Director of the Australian Museum in Sydney. Apart from copious observations and records, he produced a catalogue of watercolors of Aborigine, Māori, and African traditional life, and it is he who can be thanked for much of the visual records of Māori traditional life that exist today. He described an early Māori homestead, writing, "Sleeping or dwelling houses are partly sunk in the ground, and are always built with a gable roof and a verandah, where the occupants generally sit. The inner chamber serves as a sleeping-apartment, and towards evening is heated by means of a fire in the center; after the family enters for the night, the door and window are tightly closed, and in this almost suffocating atmosphere the inhabitants pass the night; when day comes, they creep out of the low door into the sharp morning air, dripping with perspiration."

Angas

In the early period of settlement, lifestyles were often nomadic, and homes as a consequence were at best semi-permanent. They were traditionally built in groups, with usually a simple wooden framework draped with reeds, bulrushes, or palm leaves, and occasionally with bark. Structures could be square, round, or oval, with earthen floors covered in mats, and with furnishings comprising bedding mats and little more. They were generally smaller than the typical Polynesian island style, with low doors and no windows, built often partly below ground level or heaped with earth around the sides. An interior fire usually provided for heat and cooking, with a simple opening in the roof to allow the smoke to escape. These dwellings were built in small, largely unprotected settlements known as "kainga," but by the 15th century, as settled communities began to develop, a more structured political organization was established.

One of the most striking features of traditional Māori society that whites noticed and recorded was their highly developed martial abilities. Warfare is embedded in the Māori creation myth, and a god of war, Tū or Tūmatauenga, is ubiquitous in Māori religious iconography.[2] Warfare tended to be internecine, with long traditions of conflict between groups and tribes (iwi), the origins of which were often lost over time. Indeed, by the time of the Europeans' arrival, Māori warfare had developed into a highly ritualized, almost religious observance. There are many living custodians of Māori history who will not accept the notion that Māori warfare was wanton and driven by an excess of violence, which is how the likes of Percy Smith and George French Angas were apt to describe it. Instead, it is described as simply a byproduct of a society displaying a preference for smaller, independent political and family units. Inevitably, under this social arrangement, squabbles and occasional conflagrations over land and natural resources would arise, and these, it is said, were typically resolved by diplomacy, with warfare only as a last resort.

That may well have been the case, but the imagery of warfare and the countenance of the god of war all tend to suggest a highly developed ideal of war and its associated rites of passage, and a highly theatrical tradition of martial display. The net result, regardless of what place war occupied in society, was the replacement of loosely configured and semi-nomadic kainga with fortified settlements known as pā. These ranged from simple defensive settlements to elaborate hill forts and permanent fortified villages. By then, Māori architecture had developed in sophistication, and permanent settlements and communities were a great deal more substantial. A communal sleeping house, or wharepuni, became the focus of the kainga, and therein several families could be accommodated each night. Typically, these were unadorned, although if the building happened to belong to a leader or community elder, his prestige, or "mana," might be illustrated with elaborately carved lintels (pare), pillars (poutokomanawa), or figurines (tekoteko). Often a porch or portico was included as an intermediate zone, which is a uniquely Māori adaption to the standard South Pacific communal dwelling.

---

[2] There are numerous Māori deities, some thirty-six formally listed, ranging from fire gods to sea gods, and gods governing various phases of life.

A depiction of a pā

Other buildings associated with a pā or fortified kainga was a common storehouse, pātaka, and a kāuta, or a simple outdoor kitchen.

Within these structures, a complex society resided. In classic Māori society, the largest political unit was the iwi, or tribe. Few if any examples of federations were ever recorded. Alliances were periodically formed between iwi of the same "canoe," but these were usually military alliances that were formed for the duration of a particular campaign, and rarely amounted to an authentic confederacy.[3] While the iwi was the largest political unit, it certainly was not the most important, for while individuals might give allegiance to the chief or leader of their iwi, their primary loyalty lay always with the hapū, a sub-tribe made up of extended family groups known as wahanau. The leader of a hapū was an Ariki, or chief, who derived his authority from his mana, itself inherited from his ancestors. The concept of "mana" is difficult to quantify outside of Māori idiom, and it perhaps shares superficial similarities to words such as "kismet" and "mojo" in terms of a combination of earthly rank, authority, and prestige, with more esoteric spiritual powers and inherited charisma. Mana as a concept lies very much at the heart of Māori society, and very frequently at the root of wars and conflicts. Mana is related to the concept of "utu," which is defined as reciprocation, or balance. In other words, every reaction must have an

---

[3] The Māori origin story claims the arrival of seven original canoes, or waka, from which the original identity of the tribes are drawn. To be of the same canoe implies part of the seven original iwe.

equal and appropriate reaction. If mana is greeted with kindness, utu demands kindness in return. If, however, mana is offended by violence, deceit or aggression, then utu demands similar reciprocation,which is simply revenge. That revenge, customarily, would wholly exceed the extent of the original injury, and thus utu had a tendency to proliferate and expand far beyond even the memory of the original insult or slight. It was of profound importance that an iwi's mana remain in balance, for mana was ultimately derived from the gods, and without it, an iwi was impotent in both war and peace, and would inevitably perish as a consequence.

If and when an important decision affecting the hapū required discussion, a public meeting was usually held on the marae, or village square, generally located in front of the wharerunanga or central meeting house. Here, various family heads, or kaumatua, were invited to speak, although the Ariki spoke first and last, and his decision on any matter was final.

Within society, there existed certain guilds, or tohunga, specializing in the skilled tasks associated with daily life. These, for example, could be building or woodcarving, or perhaps fishing, agriculture, hunting, or the manufacture of garments and tools. A large part of the function of a tohunga was to act as an archivist for the rituals and processes associated with a specific craft, and such rituals were central to almost every aspect of life. Each tohunga, therefore, was endowed with the function and powers of a medium or priest. Collectively, all of this was grail of tribal history, and a point of contact with Io Matua Kore, or the Supreme Being.

Absent from the built environment, however, was any kind of structure, gathering place, or large shrine to honor any religion. Indeed, Māori religion, in all of its many facets, has left very little material trace. The modest tuahu, or altars, still occasionally in use, hardly compete with the type of massive iconography associated with Easter Island or Tahiti, for example.

Another field of detailed anthropological study undertaken in the early years regarded the Māori concepts of ownership, and in the matter of proprietorship and property, it was generally believed that a kind of collectivism was practised without individual property rights at all. This has now come to be regarded as an oversimplification, and while such individual property rights were limited to possession, slaves, and occasional natural objects of spiritual importance, they were important and zealously protected. Land, however, was somewhat different. The land was Papa, the earth goddess from whom all Māori descended, so no concept of individual land ownership existed at all. The land was like the air and the water. The only avenue of land alienation was warfare and conquest, and land required occupation and tillage before it could be deemed that the correct "relationship" had been established. This, again, is an oversimplification, but the complexities of the Māori relationship with the land, notwithstanding certain common themes, tend to defy any single umbrella definition.

When the first contacts were made between European mariners and Māori and the whites observed their aggressive and warlike tendencies, they were often impressed by the Māori aptitude for trade. Intertribal and community trade was widespread, and based on the simple concept of homai o homai, or "a gift for a gift." In simple terms, an individual or delegation representing an iwi or a hapū, visiting another would bring an array of gifts, usually selected with a view to what their hosts would most appreciate. Coastal dwellers, for example, would offer fish, while inland dwellers might offer potted birds and rats. Hapū with particular artisans and skills might exchange carvings, tools, weapons or garments. None of this was conducted in the spirit of barter, but utu, requiring reciprocation, and hence an exchange, and often that reciprocation was larger and greater, requiring further reciprocation, and so on.

Thus, as Europeans appeared on the scene and began to introduce such fundamentals, as well as knives and axes, pots and mirrors, and glass beads and other decorative items, the Māori were quick to pick up the concept and willingly began to acquire and produce what was demanded in exchange. Before long, an item of magnificent utility was placed in the hands of the Māori, and soon after that, the sound of gunfire began to ring with ever-increasing frequency in the villages and valleys of both islands.

Even as Europeans grew more active around Australia and New Zealand, Captain Cook was tired of riding a desk and began looking for an excuse to go back out to sea. He found it when the Admiralty asked him to sail toward North America in search of the rumored Northwest Passage, a connection between the Atlantic and Pacific Oceans that European powers had long believed was located above the North American continent. In January 1776, Cook wrote to a friend, "For some time past I have been looking out for a ship to accompany the Resolution on her intended voyage; I expect one will be purchased tomorrow, but then I shall have to attend to the alterations which will be necessary to be made in her."

As it happened, Cook took the *Resolution* out again, and this time he was joined by Charles Clerke and HMS *Discovery*. The cause had the potential to be profitable as Parliament had promised 20,000 pounds to the person who discovered the famed passage, and the plan was for Cook to approach the passage from the Pacific while Richard Pickersgill sailed the *Lyon* from the Atlantic. They hoped to meet each other in mid-1778.

Samuel Adkin's painting of the *Resolution* and *Discovery*

Cook sailed from Plymouth on July 12, 1776, unaware that his king had just lost his 13 North American colonies. On December 13, Cook came across a group of small land masses he named after the kings's son, the Prince Edward Islands, and he subsequently sailed on to New Zealand, arriving at Queen Charlotte Sound on February 12, 1777. Omai thought it would be fun to invite some of the natives of New Zealand to join him in his homeland. He convinced one man to join him, along with a young boy whose father wanted him to go, and the two quickly regretted their decisions. Cook wrote, "They wept both in publick and in private, and made their lamentations in a kind of song which, so far as we could understand of it, was in praise of their country and people they should never see more. Thus they continued for many days, till their seasickness wore off and the tumult of their minds begun to subside, then fits of lamentation became less and less frequent and at length quite went off, so that their friends nor their native country were no more thought of, and were as firmly attached to us as if they had been born amongst us."

Cook and his crew intended to sail for Tahiti but instead ended up first at Mangaia and later at the Friendly Isles. During this time, they ran short on water, and Cook noted, "In order to save [water] I ordered the still to be kept at work from 6 in the morning to 4 in the afternoon, during which time we procured from 13 to 16 gallons of fresh water. There has lately been made some improvement, as they are pleased to call it, to this machine, which in my opinion is much for the worse."

Once on the Friendly Isles, the crew enjoyed rather good fortune and Cook was able to write that "we were not troubled with thieves of rank, their servants or slaves were employed on this dirty work, on which a flogging made no more impression than it would have done upon the main mast. Their masters, so far from making interest for them when they were caught, would very often advise us to kill them, and as this was a punishment we did not chuse to inflict, they generally escaped unpunished, because we could inflict nothing which they thought a punishment. Captain Clerke hit upon a method which had some effect, this was by shaving their heads, for though it is not a very uncommon thing to see both men and women with their heads shaved, yet its being done on this occasion was looked upon as a mark of infamy, and marked out the man."

After remaining on the Friendly Islands for nearly two months, Cook sailed on to Tahiti, where he enjoyed the honors one would expect to be given to a foreign dignitary. From there he sailed north for about five weeks before coming across a series of islands, jewels in the middle of the Pacific now known as the Hawaiian Islands. On January 18, 1778, he and his men were the first Europeans to ever see them.

HMS *Resolution* and *Discovery* in Tahiti

At the time, the Islands, which Cook called the Sandwich Islands, were just another series of landfalls, and he did not stay in the area long, instead travelling east toward the west coast of California and then north to landfall on the coast of what is now Oregon. From there he moved on to Nootka Sound on Vancouver Island, where he welcome the native peoples on board, only to later write, " Before we left the place, hardly a bit of brass was left in the ship, except what was in the necessary instruments. Whole suits of clothes were stripped of every button. Bureaux, etc., of their furniture, and copper kettles, tin canisters, candle-sticks, etc., all went to wreck, so that these people got a greater medly and variety of things from us than any other people we had visited." In spite of this, Cook still spoke well of the people he met saying, "I never found that these fits of passion went further than the parties concerned, either with us or among themselves, the others never troubled themselves about it, nay, often with so much indifference as if they did not see it. I have often seen a man rave and scold for more than half an hour without anyone taking the least notice of it, nor could anyone of us tell who it was he was abusing."

Like many Europeans, Cook was more comfortable with the aboriginal peoples in cooler climates, since they wore more clothes. He wrote of them being clothed in "skins of animals chiefly, and they also made some kind of cloth manufactured from fibre or wool and hair, or a mixture of both. In these clothes, with the addition of a coarse mat and a strong straw hat, they would sit in their canoes through the heaviest rain as unconcernedly as if they were in perfect shelter." Cook and his men travelled up the coast to the Bering Strait, along the way locating an inlet that today bears his name. Though his were among the first maps made of the North American coastline, Cook was unable to make it through the Strait. By this time his health was beginning to suffer and he may have wondered if he was getting to old to go traipsing around the globe.

Still, there were some small reliefs, such as one he described the took place around the area of what is now Alaska. "On the 8th by the hand of an Indian, Derramoushk, I received a very singular present considering the place, it was a rye loaf or rather a pie made in the form of a of us could read. We, however, had no doubt but this present was from some Russians in our neighbourhood, and sent to these our unknown friends by the same hand a few bottles of rum, wine, and porter which we thought would be as acceptable as anything we had besides, and the event proved we were not mistaken. I also sent along with Derramoushk and his party, Corporal Ledyard of the Marines, an intelligent man, in order to gain some further information, with orders, if he met with any Russians, or others, to endeavour to make them understand that we were English, Friends, and Allies."

Having had enough of cold weather, Cook turned his ship back toward the Hawaiian Islands, arriving a few weeks later but not making land until January 17, 1779. Meanwhile, the native peoples continued to row out to his ships with gifts, including large amounts of sugar cane, which he had especial need for since it could be brewed into beer. However, he also observed a problem: "[W]hen the cask came to be broached, not one of my mutinous crew would so much as taste it. As I had no motive for doing it, but to save our spirit for a colder climate, I gave myself no trouble either to oblige or persuade them to drink it, knowing there was no danger of the scurvy so long as we had plenty of other vegetables, but that I might not be disappointed in my views, I gave orders that no grog should be served in either ship. Myself and the officers continued to make use of this beer whenever we could get cane to make it; a few hops, of which we had some on board, was a great addition to it: it has the taste of new malt beer, and I believe no one will doubt but it must be very wholesome, though my turbulent crew alleged it was injurious to their health. They had no better reason to support a resolution they took on our first arrival in King George's Sound, not to drink the spruce beer we made there; but whether from a consideration that this was no new thing or any other reason, they did not attempt to carry their resolution into execution, and I never heard of it till now. Every innovation whatever, tho' ever so much to their advantage, is sure to meet with the highest disapprobation from seamen. Portable soup and sour kraut were at first both condemned by them as stuff not fit for human beings to eat. Few men have introduced into their ships more novelties in the way of victuals and drink than I have done; indeed, few men have had the same opportunity or been driven to the same necessity. It has, however, in a great measure been owing to such little innovations that I have always kept my people, generally speaking, free from that dreadful distemper, the Scurvy."

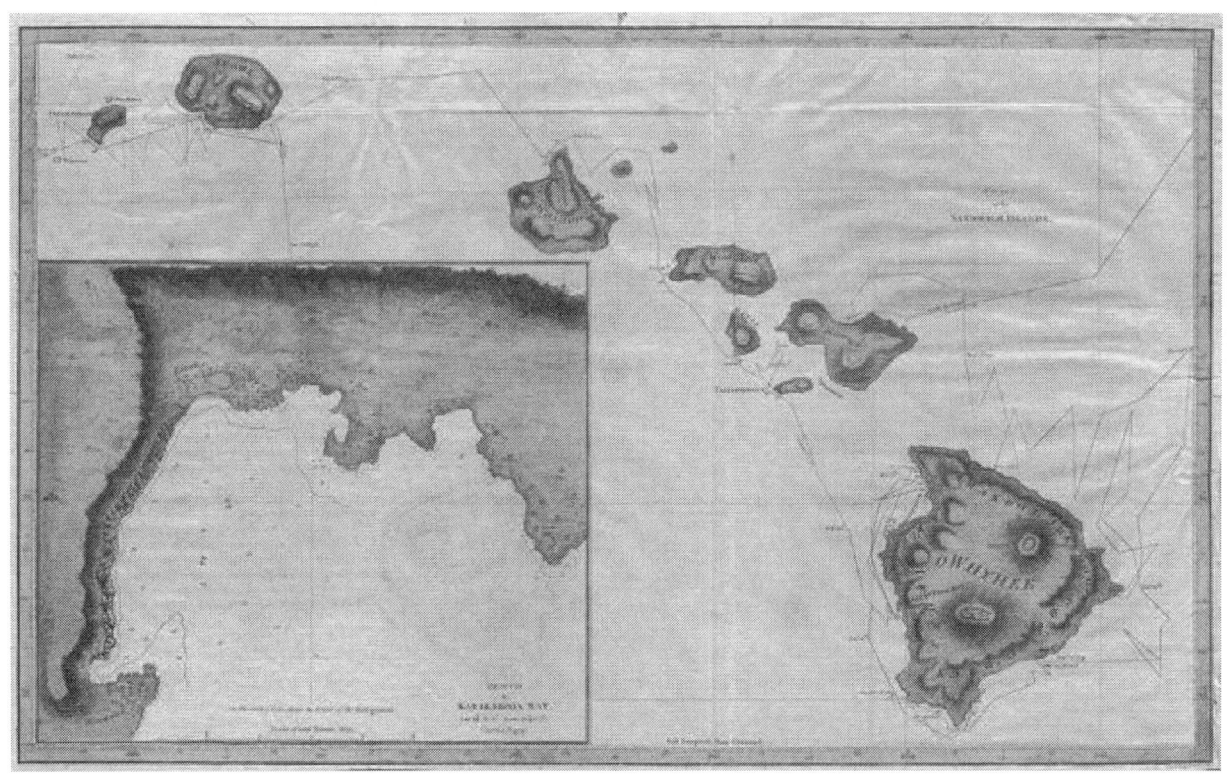

The Hawaiian Islands, by one of Cook's officers

Lithograph of a village visited by Cook near Waimea, Kauai

A View of a Morai at O'whyhee.
Published Dec. 14, 1781, by G. Robinson.

Kealakekua Bay, by William Ellis

On January 6, 1779, Cook wrote about his decision to finally send men ashore, and the interesting results: "Being near the shore I sent Mr. Bligh, the Master, in a boat to sound the coast, with orders to land and look for fresh water. On his return he reported that at two cable lengths from the shore he had no soundings with a 160 fathoms of line; that when he landed he found no fresh water, but rain water lying in holes in the rocks, and that brakish with the spray of the sea, and that the surface of the country was wholly composed of large slags and ashes, here and there partly covered with plants. Between 10 and 11 o'clock we saw the Discovery coming round the south point of the Island and at 1 P.M. she joined us, when Captain Clerke came on board and informed me that he had cruized four or five days where we were separated and then plyed round the last part of the Island, but meeting with unfavourable winds, was carried some distance from the coast. He had one of the islanders on board all the time; it was his own choice, nor did not leave them the first opportunity that offered."

A few days later, Cook made what turned out to be his final journal entry: "Sun. 17. Fine pleasant weather and variable faint breezes of wind. In the evening Mr. Bligh returned and reported that he had found a bay in which was good anchorage and fresh water, tolerable easy to come at. Into this bay I resolved to go to refit the ships and take in water. As the night approached the Indians retired to the shore, a good [many] however desired to sleep on board, curiosity was not their only motive, at least not with some of them, for the next morning several things were missing, which determined me not to entertain so many another night. At n A.M. anchored in the bay which is called by the natives (Karakakoa) in 13 fathoms of water over a sandy bottom, and a quarter of a mile from the N.E. shore. ... The ships very much crowded with Indians and surrounded by a multitude of canoes. I have nowhere in this sea seen such a number of people assembled at one place, besides those in the canoes all the shore of the bay was covered with people and hundreds were swimming about the ships like shoals of fish. We should have found it difficult to have kept them in order had not a chief or servant of Terreeoboo's, named Parea, now and then (shewn) his authority by turning or rather driving them all out of the ship. Among our numerous visitors, was a man named Touahah who we soon found belonged to the church, he introduced himself with much ceremony, in the course of which he presented me with a small pig, two cocoanuts and a piece of red cloth which he wrapped round me. In this manner all or most of the chiefs or people of note introduce themselves, but this man went further, he brought with him a large hog and a quantity of fruits and roots all of which he included in the present. In the afternoon I went ashore to view the place accompanied by Touahah, Parea, Mr. King and others; as soon as we landed Touahah took me by the hand and conducted me to a large Morai, the other gentlemen with Parea, and four or five more of the natives followed."

What Cook had no way of knowing is that he had landed on the island at the perfect time - during Makahiki, the harvest festival. He left before the festival was over, believing all was well, only to return a few weeks later during the season of battle. Just as they had once welcomed him in honor of their gods, now the native peoples sought to provoke him into battle, first by stealing one of his longboats on the night of February 13.

Taking the bait, Cook decided to kidnap the ali'I nui, the monarch of the island. He led his men from the ship to the king's home, where they captured the ruler and marched him out from where he had been sleeping. Kanekapolei's wife saw what was happening and alerted the other chiefs. Several men followed the group back to the beach, where the king finally realized that he was not being escorted to a social call. He stopped walking and sat down. As an elderly kahuna approached them, chanting, the Europeans looked up to see that the beach was full of thousands of Hawaiians.

Frightened, Cook and his men raised their weapons. One of the chiefs, Kana'ina, approached Cook, who slapped him with the flat side of his sword. The chief picked Cook up and slammed him to the ground, where another man stabbed him with a sharp dagger. Six other Europeans were either killed or wounded in the melee that followed.

Captain W.J.L. Wharton described the moment of Cook's death: "While walking down to the boat, the natives, who were momentarily increasing in numbers, implored the king not to go. His wife joined her entreaties. Taraiopu hesitated. At this moment a man ran up and cried, "It is war; they have killed a chief!" One of the guard boats had, in fact, fired at a canoe attempting to leave the bay, and killed a man. The natives at once ran to arms, and Cook, seeing his intentions frustrated, walked towards the boat. A native attacked him with a spear, and Cook shot him with his gun. Still, no further attack was made, but the men in the boats hearing Cook's shot, and seeing the excited crowd, commenced to fire without orders. Cook still moved to the shore, calling to his men to cease firing; but whilst so doing, and with his back to the exasperated natives, he was stabbed in the back with a dagger, and fell with his face in the water. There was then general confusion. The boats were a little way from the beach, and several of the marines were also killed, before they could reach them. Cook's body was at once dragged off by the natives. The boats returned on board amid general consternation, and it is mentioned that a general silence reigned on board when it was known that their beloved commander had fallen."

Death of Captain Cook by Johann Zoffany, 1795

John Webber's painting of Cook's death

Some Hawaiians also died when they were shot, but the soldiers were badly outnumbered and quickly retreated to the ship. Young William Bligh, who would later gain notoriety as the captain of HMS *Bounty*, watched in horror as the native peoples "cleaned" Cook's corpse like it was a large fish, even baking it to remove the flesh from his captain's bones. What he could not understand at the time was that the Hawaiians were actually treating Cook with respect; preparing his bones was a form of veneration that they also practiced for their own beloved leaders. The bones were even returned to the Europeans later for proper burial at sea.

Bligh

A Common System

As the Europeans' lack of familiarity makes clear, they had no idea what kind of cultures they were encountering, but that didn't stop them from coming up with theories from the moment contacts were made. Fully aware that the indigenous peoples had to travel vast distances to reach the various islands, historians and anthropologists immediately wondered how the ancient travelers knew that lands lay beyond the ocean horizon. The ocean spaces were so inconceivably vast and the specks of land that comprise the islands were so dispersed that some previous knowledge or explorations must surely have preceded the decisions to strike out with an expedition to found a new settlement. Some stories tell of the happy accident of landfall on some unexpected island, but these are surprisingly rare. Clearly, navigational prowess was so highly valued in Polynesian society that tribes were more willing to acknowledge that they were soundly defeated by a powerful chief and forced to evacuate than simply admit that they came upon the shores of a new or friendly island purely by luck.

Historians have reasonably concluded as a consequence that an ongoing process of exploration was underway well before the massive migrations actually began. In other words, when the larger expeditions set off with the essentials necessary to create a settlement, including food, livestock, and people, most had a clear idea where they were heading. Certainly, the occasional happy accident occurred, but these would have been the exception rather than the rule.

Of course, this required remarkably advanced abilities for the time. Long before Nordic and Scandinavian mariners began their probes of the outer realm of the North Atlantic, Polynesian seamen were navigating the loneliest and largest stretches of water on the globe. To achieve this, a style of large, double-hulled sailing canoes was developed, and they were sail-driven or assisted. These ships must have traveled in fleets and were capable of carrying large numbers of people. Navigational techniques developed over generations were passed down from master to apprentice, and every island and community included highly revered guilds of navigators that served as an archive for generations, indeed centuries of accumulated knowledge. The art of Polynesian navigation, therefore, was arcane, and although based on some crude instrumentation and mapping, it relied mostly on accumulated memory and oral traditions. They were also enhanced by tracking bird migrations, ocean currents, and the stars, with an almost uncanny capacity for dead reckoning, spatial awareness, and concise observation.

The culture that these migrating people carried with them incorporated hunting, fishing, animal husbandry, and simple agriculture. They took coconuts with them, and coconut trees spread through the South Pacific as a consequence, alongside the breadfruit tree, various yams and sweet potatoes, and the gourd. In fact, while there is some evidence of early pottery, that craft fell away thanks to the utility of coconut shells and gourds. Dogs were introduced to the islands, as were pigs and fowls.

Along with all of these practical things, the people developed and retained more ephemeral elements of culture and mythology. Not surprisingly, the common culture and belief system of Polynesia derived from the same fundamental spiritual stimulus as all other animist societies, most notably the Sun, Moon, the elements, and the recurring patterns and sequences of nature. While there are numerous essential commonalities that bind Polynesian mythology and folklore into one, there are also features unique to individual islands.

Common points that require a little elucidation are the concepts of mana and tapu, the latter being the origin of the word "taboo." The word originates from the Tongan tapu, or the Fijian tabu, which are related to the Māori notion of tapu and the Hawaiian kapu. In every case, the word denotes something sacred or holy, and under certain circumstances forbidden (although not necessarily prohibited or forbidden as it has come to apply in general European usage).

In his book *Te Ika a Maui*, the 19th century New Zealand missionary Richard Taylor described tapu: "This singular institution, which pervades the entire extent of Polynesia, may perhaps be correctly defined as a religious observance, established for political purposes. It consisted in making any person, place or thing sacred for a longer or shorter period." Tapu might, for example, reinforce the authority of kings or priests while at the same time preserve a particular dwindling reserve of fish or coconuts. It has been noted that when European missionaries arrived in the South Pacific and began diluting traditional systems and values, previously well-preserved stocks of lagoon fish began to decline.

The word mana has been similarly adapted by common English and European use. At its root, it describes another uniquely Polynesian concept, the supernatural force or power contained within gods, people, and inanimate objects. It has been suggested that the common vernacular term "mojo," implying some supernatural capability or an advanced, messianic charisma, is a comparable concept. Mana can also be described as a spiritual energy that can be gained or lost, and as such it is defined by actions and behaviors. In Māori culture, mana has a more definitive meaning within a warlike culture, implying prestige, authority, and charisma. Mana lost in battle, for example, can be retrieved only by revenge or retaliation. In general, however, anthropologists make a point of avoiding a definitive description of mana, admitting that the elusive allegory of myth and folklore tends to do a better job of explaining it.

Then there is kura, meaning approximately the color red, inclusive of the ochres of clay as well as the brilliant red of a bird's plumage. Perhaps most importantly, red is also the color of blood. Captain Cook took note of the particular fondness for red among the people who he encountered, and that observation was echoed by many other writers and scholars. This can perhaps be explained by an almost complete absence of red in the natural palette of blue, green, and white, so red was associated with such ethereal events as sunrise and sunset, not to mention the spiritually potent blood.

Ultimately, the importance of kura began to erode once Europeans determined its desirability and began introducing red garments and artifacts as trade items.

Around the 13th century, the mass migrations were finished, and it became known that no more habitable islands remained to be discovered. A common belief system then evolved that the origin of the disparate peoples of Polynesia was a legendary homeland island known as Havaiki or Hawaiki. Hawaiki, with variations, features prominently in the mythology of every branch of the Polynesian race. Among the Māori and Marquesas islanders, Hawaiki is associated with the underworld and death.

Finally, scholars have noted that among the various collections of stories and myths, there are frequent allusions to sexuality, sex, and cannibalism. There has certainly tended to be a sense that both cannibalism and sexual liberalism infused Polynesian society before the arrival of the Christian missionaries, and it is true that the theme is commonly espoused in every branch of Polynesian folklore. There is without a doubt much truth in the popular perception of Polynesian sexual freedom, although some early historians have remarked that the uninhibited hospitality enjoyed by English sailors in Tahiti was not altogether removed from what waited for them in any port anywhere, and the transactional aspects of it would certainly have been comparable. In traditional Polynesian society, sexual liberty was common enough, but only before marriage. After marriage, monogamy tended to prevail.

The fact that sexual freedom lacked the same "taboo" as it did in Victorian England ought not to detract from the more evident modesties of Polynesian life, and the many closely followed protocols of behavior and the treatment of one another. An interesting observation was made by early missionaries, who were, ironically, the first to create a written record of indigenous society and customs at the same time they were trying to break them down. With regards to the use of words describing male and female genitalia and the excretory organs, it was considered offensive to refer to any of them directly, but rather by metaphor. A penis, for example, might be referred to as a "needle," and a vulva simply as a "thing," while the sexual act might be referred to as "doing the sacred thing." Obscene gestures were largely absent in Polynesian society, and although profanity did exist, it was rarely if ever used to inflict personal insult.

Cannibalism certainly existed (and continues to exist) in the folklore of almost every Polynesian culture, but it seems as though the practice was beginning to fall out of custom by the time Europeans began arriving on the scene. Alongside their crusades against drumming, dancing, polygamy, and superstition, European missionaries tried to stamp out any hint of cannibalism wherever it was suspected.

As a practice, it tended to be confined only to certain islands and was never based on dietary needs. There was a notion widespread among Polynesians that close to the lowest order of things was cooked food – not what comes out of the body, but what goes into it – which then goes some way to explain the ritual practice of eating an enemy. If this was true (and it would have been truer in some places than others), then the act of cannibalism can be regarded as the ultimate obscenity. Warfare was a common enough event throughout Polynesia, and it grew almost to the dimension of a national obsession among the Māori. Indeed, the stigma of cannibalism remains very heavy over the history and legacy of the Māori, while Fiji, another island full of warlike tribes, was known to early European visitors as "Cannibal Island."

The subject is one of extreme delicacy in New Zealand today where cultural historians will admit only to the fact that cannibalism was practiced as part of the protocol of war, as a means primarily of revenge, and involving only prisoners of war. Nowhere has it been established that cannibalism was practiced as a dietary preference, and popular tales that human flesh was prized as a delicacy above all others are simply that. In an observation made in his 1910 book *Melanesians and Polynesians*, the missionary and ethnographer George Brown noted, "When a group of Samoans went to beg pardon for any offence, they bowed down in front of the offended chief's house, and each man held in his hand a small bundle of firewood, some leaves, stones, and earth. These were symbolic of the deepest humiliation and meant: 'Here we are, the people who have so deeply sinned. And here are the stones, the firewood and leaves and earth to make the oven in which you can cook us, and eat us, if it be your will.' In most cases the offended chief would come out of his house with a fine mat in his hand, which he would give to the suppliants, 'to cover their disgrace.'"

Creation and Origin

In the beginning, according to the islanders of French Polynesia, there was none but Ta'aroa, the creator of all things, himself among them. Inside his egg he waited, a capsule of sorts spinning in an empty and lifeless void. This was the time before the earth, and before the sun, moon and stars. There was only Ta'aroa incubating alone in the void. At a certain time, growing bored, and feeling that the time was right, he cracked his shell and emerged. Looking around, he perceived himself alone in the desolation, for everything around him was silent and empty.

He shattered his shell into many pieces, and from the shards, he fashioned the rocks and the sand, the essential elements of the physical world. He looked around, and he was pleased with his work, but still it was incomplete. With his spine he created the mountains and from his tears came the oceans. With his fingernails he created the scales that cover the bodies of fish and from his feathers came the trees and the shrubs. And with his blood, that most sacred of elements, he tinted the colors of the rainbow.

He then called out for artists to sculpt Tane, the first of the Gods.[4] Tane was followed by Ru, Hina and Maui, and a great many others besides.[5] Although it was Tane who populated the heavens with a sun, a moon and stars, it was Ta'aroa himself who created man.

The world was then separated into seven levels. On the lowest level, man resided, and there he multiplied quickly which pleased Ta'aroa. However, man soon felt constrained within the limits of his world, which he shared with the fish and the animals, and he cut a hole in his own level to infiltrate another, and then another until eventually all the world was populated by men. The whole, however, remained the dominion of Ta'aroa who returned to the void leaving earth to its prosperity.

The first man was born of a union between Te Tumu and Ahuone, both of whom were atuas, or supernatural beings. He was born in the shape of a round ball which his father molded and refashioned into the form of a human being, calling him then O Ti'i, or "Finished." O Ti'i lay with his mother and from her was born a daughter named Hina I 'ere'ere nonai. Hina I 'ere'ere nonai was initiated by her father into the same mysteries, and soon gave birth to Hina i o wai, with whom O Ti'i also visited, fathering Hina i ta'a ta'a. She too O Ti'i impregnated, creating Hina rorohi. By the same sequence there came Hina nui ta'i te marama, and then a son Taha i te ra'i, who, with his mother, fathered a son 'Oro and a daughter Hina i pia who together begot Ana, another son. From these three men and the women came forth all of mankind.

The above story is told in multiple variations, but it can justly be regarded as the essential Polynesian creation myth. It was the first to be recorded by a European, and as the story goes, it was told either to Captain James Cook in Tahiti, or his companion Sir Joseph Banks, the eminent geographer and scholar, and later president of the Royal Geographic Society. The date of its transcription was probably 1769, and it resides in the notes of Captain Cook housed today in the archive of the Royal Navy. A common variation is the existence of a sky god, or a sky-father, and an earth-mother who between them produce numerous sons who then occupy positions as departmental gods, one of whom is tasked to separate his parents in order to allow light to enter upon the world of being. There soon arrives a first man, and then a first woman.

---

[4] *Tane* is described by Sir George Grey, Prime Minister and third Governor of New Zealand as *"...the god of forests and of birds, and the son of Ranginui and Papatūanuku, the sky father and the earth mother, who used to lie in a tight embrace where their many children lived in the darkness between them."*

[5] *Hina* is a term that appears regularly in Polynesian mythology. It is the name applied to many deities and female characters.

One such version, taken from the Chatham Islands, tells of Rangi and Papa, common enough names across the cultural spectrum who represent respectively the Sky and the Earth. In the beginning, there was only darkness, for Rangi adhered so closely over his wife Papa. Then there arose a person, indeed, a spirit without origin and his name was Rangitokona, the "Supporter-of-Heaven." Rangitokona approached Rangi and Papa and asked them to separate, in order that light might enter between them, but they refused. Rangitokona then thrust the two apart, installing Rangi up above, and holding him there with ten pillars. So grieved was Rangi at this separation from Papa that his tears flowed, falling upon Papa as rain. For the first time, however, there was light, for now there was space between the earth and the sky.

When this was done, Rangitokona gathered up a heap of earth, and from this, he made a man, who was named Tu, and who was given the life spirit in the form of a white bird, and by means of a sneeze. Thus, man existed and multiplied.

A similar version, also derived from Tahiti, tells of Ta'aroa living within his shell in the empty void until that moment when he cracked it and stood up, looking around.

"Who is above and who is below?" he called out, but all was silent.

"Who is in front and who is behind?" Still, no voice answered.

He commanded a rock to crawl to him, but it would not. He commanded the sand to do likewise, and it would not. By this indifference to his authority, Ta'aroa was enraged, and he overturned his shell, creating from it the sky which he named Rumia, meaning "Overturned."

Then from his backbone, he created the mountains and from his ribs the descending ridges and valleys. He took his guts, and from them created the clouds. From his flesh he created the bounty of the earth, and his arms and legs its strength and vitality. His fingernails became the scales and shells of fish and his feathers the trees and plants. From his blood came the colors of the sunrise and the sunset, and after that, everything that is red is derived from Ta'aroa's blood. His head, however, remained sacred to himself. He was master of all that he created, all that is, and below him his creation multiplied.

From the Tuamotu Archipelago in French Polynesia comes the story of a conflict between the gods, another common variant of the creation myth. Atea is a Polynesian deity present in several cultures, including New Zealand, the Marquesas and Tuamotu. When first he existed, he was without tangible form, and thus he remained until the enchantress Vahine Nautahu, through the utterance of a chant, molded him into a pleasing shape. After that he became the god of the sky, or the expanse lying above the third layer of the world. His wife was Fakahotu, and between them they had many sons, and Fakahotu gave birth to all of the creatures of the earth.

Tane was the son of Te hau and Metua, and he resided with his parents and ancestors in the paradise known as Vavau. At a certain time, Tane and his people came down to make war on Atea, but they were defeated by his army. Many were killed, some escaped, but Tane found himself left behind. Sensing this danger, he dropped below to live among the humans, and there he became enamored of food, a thing which did not exist in his realm.

When Atea learned that the young god was sojourning on the earth below, he placed sentries at every corner to prevent his return, but Tane was skillful in evading them, and he moved between the realms with ease. In heaven, where his parents believed him dead and mourned his death, he discovered that there was no food to be had, and so he killed one of his ancestors and ate him, from whence the tradition of men eating of men began. As he grew to maturity, in the meanwhile, Tane vowed revenge on Atea. From his ancestor Fatu-tiri, who was thunder, he was given lightning, and with this as a weapon, he assembled an army. His father told him that should he witness on earth ants gathered around the stump of a tree, feeding upon its flowers, the time would be right to plant his seeds, and he would know what to do.

When this came to pass when Tane did see ants thus engaged, he planted the seeds of a Pia bush which grew large and quickly, and upon it he rose and extended to the heavens, fixing the earth and the sky in their proper places. As he did, the Pia remained on the lowest layer of earth, holding up the world. When Atea saw this, he was angry, asking how it might be expected that he kneel before one who was seeking his blood. He then gathered his own army, and the two-faced one another across the plains of heaven. Tane, however, wished to kill his enemy with his own hands, and so one day he approached Atea with the curious request that he make fire.

Atea obliged, and taking up his fire plough and the grooved wooden plate, he began to rub the two together until the kindling glowed and began to smoke. As it did, Tane filled his lungs with wind and blew it away. Atea tried again, and again Tane blew it away. Frustrated and angry, Atea handed Tane the implements and told him to make fire, and now that he knew how, he did.

The flames lit the heavens, and with the lightning given to him, Tane struck Atea, killing him. His body was placed in a canoe with the name *A toa e rur ai hau*, and carried away. Atea's mana, however, was indestructible, and it survived, and it remained great in the islands where it descended to men.

Tane now had the gift of fire.

Another ubiquitous "first man" hero is Tiki, found in various guises throughout Polynesia. A version of the common Tiki tale is one commonly related in the islands Tuamotu, Mangareva and the Marquesas. As the story is told, when Tiki was born on the distant island of Hawaiki, he was set apart by Atea himself as the vessel to bring forth all of the children of mankind in the realms below. One day, when he was still young, he was instructed by his parents to play outside the house, for he was a boisterous and unruly child. For a while he did as he was told, but presently he grew bored, came back in, and there he witnessed his parents at their own enjoyment. The effect of it was curious, and he wanted the same. From a mound of earth, he created the shape of a woman, and he did with it what he had seen his father do with his mother. The woman thus created, whose name was Hina-one, he took as his wife.

The first child born to the couple was a human girl, and she was named Tiaki-te-keukeu. One day, in search of fire, Hina one went below and gave birth to the twins Kuri and Kuro who did not know their father. Tiki remained in Hawaiki with his daughter, and since it was unseemly for him to openly have her, he built for her a house in a secluded place. When it was finished, he sent her there with instructions that when she reached that place, she would encounter a being who looked like her father in every way but was not. Tiaki te keukeu left to find the place, and as she did, Tiki hurried by another way to be there before her. He greeted her when she arrived, and seduced her, and while she knew that he was her father, and resisted, she was persuaded.

Eventually, however, disgust overcame her, and she left that world to find her mother down below. When told the story, Hina one was outraged, and between the two women, they conceived a plan to kill Tiki. His sons, however, Kuri and Kuro, who did not know him, discovered the plot, and secretly arranged for another man who resembled Tiki to be summoned to Hina one's homestead. When the unfortunate man arrived, it was he who was set upon and eaten by the women.

Clearly, Tiki was as wily and resourceful and he was disreputable, and while the tales of Tiki are many and varied, in almost every one he is guilty of some similar act of licentiousness, jealousy or avarice. One day, Tiki told his beautiful daughter Tiaki that he would leave home early to go fishing, and that she was to follow him to the beach a few hours later, and to bring a basket to carry home the fish that he intended to catch. Tiaki did as she was told, and as the sun rose, she gathered up her basket and made her way down to the beach. There she noticed something protruding from the sand, and assuming that it was a particular type of stick commonly used to string fish, she reached down and pulled it. Tiki, who had covered his body with sand, leapt up. When his daughter saw who it was, and that her father was naked before her, and what she was holding in her hand, she was revolted, and she told him so. It was for this reason, as the story goes, that Tiki acquired the nicknames "Tiki the slimy," the "rigid" or the "trickster."

The trickster in Tiki's nature is well revealed in the tale of Tiki the two men. It was often said of Tiki that he was indeed not one, but two men, sometimes many more. One was handsome and the other one ugly, another sweet and yet another cruel, one conniving and the other honest. Women, it would seem, were particularly susceptible to this. Tiki could appear to them first as a driveling lunatic, flatulating and exposing himself, driving them to such a pitch of fury that they hunted him down to kill him. Tiki adored the chase, and he would run off, loping like an ape until they caught up with him. Then he would simply transform himself to become handsome Tiki, smiling and charming of character, and they would desire him, and so he would have them.

It was said that Tiki stored all his ugly features in his anus, removing them only when he wished to wear them.

One day, when Tiki appeared among the villagers in his evil form, he was seized and held down. People tried to take out his eyes, but they were unable to. They seized his tongue and tried to tie a knot in it, but it unraveled and slipped free. They cut off his ears, but he stuck them back, and they cut off his *"ure,"* or his penis, and that he returned it to its place too. When they tried to kick his teeth out, he returned them one by one, and when they tore out his eye he blinked, and they were back. They cut off his legs, and then his arms, and pulled out his guts, and rubbed off his skin with coral. As they did all this, they also built a clay oven, and built a fire, intending to cook and eat him.

Then, without warning, the loathsome Tiki was gone the handsome and kind Tiki was among them. As usual, the rage of the women was quelled, and they again desired him, and they took him, but suddenly, as they were upon him in their rapture, Tiki was ugly again, and again they set upon him, tearing him to pieces. After three repetitions of this, each one the same, he grew bored with the game and disappeared. A few hours later he was to be found asleep on the beach. Out of the water a great eel emerged and seized upon his foot. Tiki woke in a state of terror and called to his wife. Hina one hurried down to the beach and a tugging match ensued between the woman and the eel, until, quite suddenly, Tiki disappeared, leaving Hina and the eel facing one another with nothing in between.

The eel is a curious creature in Polynesian mythology. In a land without harmful snakes or insects, the symbol of treachery and evil, typically played by the snake in many cultures, is played in Polynesia by the eel. This is by no means always the case, as the following tale of "Hina and the Eel" will prove. This story originates from the Cook Islands, and it portrays the eel in another of its common roles, that of seducer, and sometimes rapist. The lithe and phallic texture and appearance of eels is commonly emphasized, and the eel is quite often portrayed as a spiritual organ providing pleasure to the body and the senses. The story of Hina and the Eel contains many of the by now familiar elements of Polynesian mythology – the flexibility of shape and form and an emphasis on personal pleasure and gratification – telling also the story of the first eel whose name was Tuna.

Hina-moe-aitu was young and beautiful. She was the daughter of Kui the blind, and it was her habit every evening to bathe in a pool at the base of the cliffs near her home. In that pool, there lived many eels, including one of great size who was Tuna. One day as she was bathing, Tuna came out from his hiding place under the rocks and swum close to her, startling her with his soft touches. Hina, however, allowed him to continue, and it did, and in the days that followed, it happened many times. Then, one day, the eel changed its shape, and emerged from the pool as a handsome young man, proclaiming himself "Tuna," god of all eels. He explained to Hina-moe-aitu that it was only his love for her that convinced him to change his shape and leave the pool.

The two lovers returned to the village, and there Tuna was careful to hide his presence by reverting to the shape of an eel whenever a person came by. The two lived together, and their love was strong.

One day Tuna told Hina-moe-aitu that he must return to his pool, and in the form of an eel, and to comfort her, he told her that a great thing would soon happen. The rain would come that night and the land would be flooded, and then he would leave his pool and swim to her bedside. When she awoke, she would find him there. She was then to take the sacred adze of her ancestors and cut off his head, and bury it at a certain place.

Sure enough, the next day a powerful rainstorm broke, and after the first fury of thunder and lightning, the rain fell steadily for many days. The countryside was flooded, and it happened precisely as he told her. One morning, as if in a dream, he appeared at her bedside. She took up the adze and cut off his head, burying it where he instructed her. Days passed and she watched carefully, and sure enough, one day a shoot rose from the spot, and then another until before long a grove of coconut trees stood in that place. This was indeed a great thing, for those trees provided food, milk and oil; leaves for baskets and roofs, and many other purposes besides. Since that day the people have called the flesh of the coconut "Tuna's Brains," and when the husk of the nut is all removed, the face of Tuna, the god of eels, his two eyes and mouth, can clearly be seen.

So much for Tuna, and the origin of the coconut. On the island of Pora-Pora in French Polynesia, the origin of pigs, fowls and turtles is attributed to Tu moana puaka, his wife Rifarifa, and their son Metua puaka, known also as the "Pig-parent." The family lived in Hawaiki, and one day, when Tu and his wife were visiting the islands of Papua, she gave birth to a brace of turtles that crawled down the beach and swam away, reproducing throughout the islands. Returning to Hawaiki, the same thing happened, but this time the couple's offspring were chickens who were released onto the land, and there, they too proliferated and multiplied. Thus, all the chickens and turtles of the world originated from this source.

Then, it so happened that a chicken and turtle met one day on a footpath, and began to argue. To the chicken the turtle said, "You are common, and will remain so, and will be eaten by women and children, while my flesh will be revered, and reserved for the table of the gods. I will leap into the house of the gods." To this, the chicken clucked a sharp retort: "How can you do that? It is you who is common and will be eaten by women and children. I will live in the deep ocean and never be caught and eaten."

At that moment a young man came by and seeing the curious turtle, he picked it up and took it to the king of all the land. So pleased was the king with this strange and beautiful gift that he sent it to the *marae*, or the shrine, where it was offered up as a gift to the gods. In this way it was the turtle who became *tapu*, to be eaten only by kings and gods.

On seeing the fate of the turtle, however, the chicken, fearing for her life, ran off to hide in the sea. No sooner had she reached the water's edge, however, than she was seized by a group of children running ahead of their mother who was gathering shellfish in the shallows. The chicken was taken home, killed, plucked, cooked and eaten, and so it was that the chicken became the common food of women and children.

Only one child resembling a human was born to Tu and Rifarifa, and that was Metua puaka. One day the parents took their sun to Pora-Pora to marry a girl that they had chosen for him. Metua had nothing to take as property so his mother told him to go into the forest and open his mouth wide, and into it would rush a great many small animals. He was to then build a stone pen and place all of the animals in it, and when he returned the following day, he would find them grown. Metua's new wife was very pleased when she saw the livestock her new husband brought, and all the pigs of the lands came from those kept by Metua.

In Tahiti, the origin of the moon is explained by the story of Hina beating tapa cloth late at night as a gift for the sea god Tangaroa.[6] The pounding of her mallet kept the great god awake, however, and he sent Pani to ask her to stop. Pani did as she was told, but returned to report that Hina would not heed, and the beating of the mallet continued. Three times Pani was sent upon this errand, and three times the request was refused. Maddened by this, Pani seized the mallet and beat Hina to death. Her spirit rose to the heavens, however, and every night she can be witnessed in the sky, beating white tapu, known from then on as Great-Hina-beating-in-the-moon.

In many Polynesian folktales, Tiki, Tane, and another character whom we will meet in a moment, Maui, were all related in various ways to the sun, and to the sun god. In Samoan mythology, the sun god is known as Tagaloa, and he is the supreme being, or the central cosmic force responsible for all things. The sun is typically the most potent symbol in all animist religion and mythology epitomized best by the Egyptian sun god Ra, and for obvious reasons. The sun is the alpha and omega, the source of all life. The emergence of Jesus Christ in the form of the sun defined the transition of many shamanistic societies into Christian. In Polynesian mythology there is an absence of origin stories for the sun, for it was in itself the origin of life.

One day, Tagaloa looked down from his place in the heavens and decided that he would like to have a place to rest on earth. From heaven, he rolled down a boulder, creating an island known as Manu'atele, or "the great wound." Pleased with his work, Tagaloa smashed Manu'atele into many smaller pieces, creating the archipelago of islands of Fiji and the Samoan chain. He then cast down a sacred vine that grew to cover the islands, breeding a curious species of worm without limbs, and without mana, or the essential spirit of life. To these inert creatures, Tagaloa gifted heads, hands and feet, and to each a beating heart, and thus were created men. Tagaloa took a male and female of each, and to each couple he gave an island. Soon it became clear that

---

[6] *Tapa* cloth is created from beating the bark of the paper mulberry tree with a wooden mallet.

the people of the islands needed kings, and so he created the sacred office of *Tui*, or "king," along with the titles of *Tuiaga'e, Tuita'u, Tuiofu, Tuiolosega, Tuiatua, Tuia'ana, Tuitoga,* and *Tuifit*. In this way he created the lords and rulers of the various islands. To rule over them all he chose the firstborn of night and day. When this child was born, it was then that he was attached by the abdomen to his mother's womb, and thus the islands that he rules acquired the name of Samoa, or the "sacred abdomen."

Heroes and Tricksters

Heroes are a universal character in human storytelling and mythology, and typically they are men or women who triumph in some way over both adversity and obstacles. Although neither immortal nor divine, they nonetheless, although it might not always be obvious, represent the best of what it means to be human. Usually they demonstrate strength, courage, wisdom, resourcefulness and devotion. The archetypical hero is the Greek hero, often a warrior gifted with both virtue and courage although the character and attributes of mythological heroes vary widely from culture to culture. Polynesian heroes, however, display not only attributes of virtue, but also trickery, jealousy, licentiousness and cunning. In many respects this is an acute observation of human nature, and it might fairly be observed that Polynesian heroes are more human in their attributes than any other.

The most widely dispersed Polynesian hero is Maui, described often as a demigod, which implies that he was part god and part human. Descriptions of Maui tend to change with geography. Maui was responsible, among many other gifts to the world, for ordering the universe, stealing fire from the underworld for the use of humans, and fishing up the islands with his magic hook, all the while engaging in rascally behavior and blatant trickery.

One of the earliest hero stories begins with Ataraga, the father of Maui and all of his brothers. When he was still young and handsome, Ataraga left his home and wandered in the forest searching for just the right timbers to build the bargeboards of his house. On the way, as he passed a popular bathing pool, he happened to encounter two young women Hina uru and Hina hava.

Ataraga truly was a very handsome man, and the two women desired him and suggested that all three return to the pool to bathe together. Although Ataraga agreed, he hurried on ahead, and when he reached the pool, he hid and waited. Soon the two girls arrived and wondered where he was, but they disrobed and entered the water anyway. As he lay hidden, he watched and listened, smiling as the girls giggled and laughed, talking about the pleasure he might have given them, one at a time or together. Then one asked the other what she thought he would do if he ever saw the lovely Huahega at the pool, and they both agreed that he would never be able to resist such divine beauty.

Ataraga was intrigued by this, and he stepped out of his hiding place to reveal himself to the women. He asked who Huahega was, and how he could meet her. They replied, "If you will take us first, then we will offer you to Huahega afterwards."

To this he agreed, and after Ataraga bathed, the three walked into the forest together. The two women were servants of Huahega, and when it was done, as they had promised, they lead Ataraga to the village of their mistress. Instructing him to wait, they approached her threshold and entered. Huahega commanded them to sit, and then asked where they had been all morning. To this, they replied that they had been at the bathing pool when they were frightened by an enormous eel.

When she heard this, Huahega was skeptical, and expressed her amazement, for she had never seen a great eel with slit skin in that particular pool although she had bathed in it since childhood. It was agreed then that the three women would investigate this curious phenomenon in the morning.

The two then hurried back to Ataraga and told him what had been arranged. The next day, Ataraga went to the pool, and there indeed he saw the beautiful Huahega dancing with her two servants, in a dance called the Dance of Hawaiki. Ataraga was enchanted, and Huahega found the great eel with the split skin. Later, Ataraga went into the forest and found just the right timbers to build the bargeboards of his house.

We return now to Maui, that strange creature of Polynesian myth and legend, the demi-god trickster who is always up to some mischief. The tales of Maui are spread widely across Polynesia, with the single common theme that, while his antics might be amusing, intriguing and often irritating, they were rarely without some unexpected benefit to mankind.

Maui is a central character of Māori myth and legend, and it is the Māori version of Maui's birth and lineage that we will tell today. Maui was born to Taranga, fathered by Makeatutara, guardian of the underworld. The child was born prematurely, delivered by the seashore, and afraid of the omens of his early birth, Taranga cut off a length of her hair, wrapped the baby in it and tossed it into the waves, offering it to Tangaroa, god of the ocean.

Tangaroa accepted the child, but seeing that he was strong, and would not die, he sent him back. There he lay on the beach, naked and vulnerable until a jellyfish wrapped itself around him to protect him from the flies and the gulls that would kill him. There he was later found by the old man, Tame-nui-ke-ti-Rangi, who took him home.

Time passed and the child grew, acquiring the powers of magic and divining, until, one day, Tame-nui-ke-ti-Rangi took him aside and told him that their time together was over. It was time for him to go and find his family. For this Maui changed his shape to a bird, and flew over the land and ocean, finding eventually his mother dancing in the house of the great tribal assembly. In that place he took his seat beside his four brothers, and when his mother apprehended five sons and not four, she named them each – Maui-taha, Maui-roto, Maui-pae, Maui-waho. Who, she then asked, was the fifth?

"I am your son too," replied Maui. "I am Maui-the-baby."

Taranga would not believe it until Maui told her the story of his birth: his sacrifice to the ocean wrapped in his mother's hair, and his return. She then believed him, and named him Maui-tikitiki-a-Taranga, or "Maui-formed-in-the-topknot-of-Taranga's hair." And so it was that Maui found his mother and his brothers.

The tales of Maui that issued from this very often have an epic flavor, and for a taste of that, the first we will hear is a story commonly told in the Cook Islands. Maui Muri resided then in the land of Rarotonga, the place of the ancestors of Manihiki, an atoll of the Cook Island chain. Manu-ahi-whare was his father and Tongo-i-ware his mother, and both were progeny of the god Tangaroa-of-the-tattooed-face.

A game the children would often play was hide and seek, and one day Maui was hidden by his sister under a pile of sticks and leaves outside the house, and although the others searched high and low, they could not find him. His sister laughed, and pointed to the pile of sticks and leaves, for there is where she had hidden him. When she looked closely, however, she was astonished to see that both Maui and the pile had disappeared. It was then that everyone knew that Maui Muri had unusual powers.

Maui Muri was his father's favorite, and each night he slept close to Manu-ahi-whare. Every morning, however, when he awoke, his father was never to be found, returning only at dusk when it was time to sleep. While the knowledge of where he went, or how he reappeared was *tapu*, Maui was determined to discover. One night he did not sleep, but instead kept vigil as his father rose before dawn and stood before a house-post at the edge of the room, uttering the chant, "O you house-post, open, open up! Open so that Manu-ahi-whare may enter, may descend to the world below."[7]

Then, a hole appeared in the floor of the room, into which Manu-ahi-whare stepped, and disappeared. Maui turned over and slept, but later that morning when the children went out to play, he went to the house-post and repeated the same chant, and sure enough a hole opened. Without thought or hesitation he stepped in. He then entered the body of a bird which flew him through the darkness to the light, and to the place where his father was. There he also found an ancient woman who was stooped over a fire with a pair of tongs trying to find the meat roasting among the coals.

Her name was Hina-porari, or Hina-the-blind, and when he spoke to her, she peered in his direction. She asked his name, but he would not tell although he was sorry for her blindness.

---

[7] Alpers, Antony. *Legends of the South Seas*. (Thomas Y Crowell & Co. New York. 1970) p93

Instead, he took up a stick and struck it against one of four *nono* trees that were growing nearby. By this, the old woman was irritated and asked who it was who struck the tree of Maui-the-first. Maui said nothing but struck the next tree, and again the woman cried, asking who it was who struck the tree of Maui-roto. Maui then struck the third tree, discovering that it was the tree of his sister Hina-ika. Then he struck the fourth tree, and discovered that it was his own.

Who, the old woman asked, is striking the sacred tree of Maui muri, the last-born child here in the underworld?

And at last, to the great surprise of the old woman, Maui revealed himself after which she revealed to him that she was his grandmother and that this indeed was his tree.

Maui climbed up the nono tree and plucked a fruit, and biting off a piece, he spat it into the old woman's eye. Suddenly, although she smarted from the pain, she could see from that eye. He did the same with the other, and the old woman's blindness was gone. In exchange, the old woman, who was once called Hina-porari, gave Maui all of the knowledge of the underworld, and the power of the world above.

She omitted one detail, however, that which intrigued Maui the most. Who was the god from whom fire was given, and to this she answered Tangaroa-tui-mata, or Tangaroa-of-the-tattooed-face, who was Maui's ancestor. Two roads existed to the house of Tangaroa, she told him, the first was the common road, taken by the living, and the second the road of the dying. It was the road of the living that the old woman instructed Maui to take.

To this Maui solemnly agreed, but he took the road of the dying instead, for contrary was his nature. As he approached, Tangaroa observed him, noticing a small person who approached by the road of the dying. Thus, he raised his hand to kill him, for no man who approached by that route could hope to survive. Maui, however, raised his hand, and Tangaroa was amazed. He raised his foot, and in reply, Maui simply raised his. He was unconcerned, and unawed.

When asked his name, Maui replied, "I am Maui muri, son of Manu-ahi-whare and Tongo-i-whare. I have come."

Tangaroa knew then that he faced his grandson, and they greeted one another with the *hongi*.[8]

When asked what he had come for, Maui replied that he wanted fire. Tangaroa gave him a burning brand and sent him away. Maui, however, did not want merely fire, but the method of fire. When he passed beside a stream of water, he threw the stick in. This he did three times, returning each time to Tangaroa for another until all the burning sticks were gone. Tangaroa then fetched two sticks and set about making fire. Each time the tinder began to smolder, however, Maui puffed and blew it away until eventually Tangaroa drove him away.

---

[8] *Hongi* is a traditional Polynesian greeting involving touching noses and foreheads.

Instead, Tangaroa called on his pet tern, a beautiful white-faced creature, to hold the grooved piece of wood while he worked the plough, and soon enough there was fire. Maui was angered by this, and he fetched up the charred firestick and threw it at the bird, leaving two black marks on its clean, white face, and so it was, and so it is to this day, that the terns of the South Seas are marked with a black brow above and below the eye.

Maui returned to his parents and showed them the secret of making fire.

The Maori version of Maui's acquisition of the secret of fire is quite different. Rather than journey to the edge of the volcano to gather embers, Maui decided that he would bring the fire to him. He knew of a race of birds that had mastered the art of creating fire so he captured their leader and forced the birds to reveal how fire was made. It was they who taught him to rub two sticks together in order to create a flame, and it was in this way that fire came to serve humanity.

One day, in the meanwhile, it occurred to Maui that the days were far too short. The sun, it appeared to him, raced across the sky with little regard for the work of men, the cooking and childcare of women, and the play of children. Maui decided that he would find a way to make the sun move more slowly, and more reasonably across the sky. He set about weaving a stout rope from coconut fiber, and from this, he fashioned a noose which he laid as a trap at the entrance to the pit out of which the sun rose. The sun, however, when caught in the noose, was far too strong and snapped the rope easily. Maui spun another, much stronger rope, but again, it was easily singed and burned by the exuberant sun. Maui then cut the sacred hair of his sister Hina, and from it he wove an enchanted rope whose mana could not be destroyed by the sun.

The sun came up that morning, emerging from the spirit world, hurrying as it rose above the horizon. Maui tugged on the rope, and this time, though the sun screamed and struggled, it could not escape. After a while it ceased to struggle, and from it Maui extracted a promise that if he were to release it, it would travel more slowly across the sky. Since that day, the days have been longer, and strands of Hina's sacred hair can still be seen radiating from the face of the sun.

Hawaiian legend has it that Maui created all of the islands of the archipelago using only his magic fish hook. Maui was the smallest of his brothers, but also the wisest and most cunning. On one particular day, when he went fishing with them, he tricked them by stealing their fish and pretending they were his own, until, in the end, they refused to allow him to fish with them anymore.

Taking pity on him, his mother told him about a secret, magical fish hook attached to the sky that had the power to raise land from the bottom of the sea. By many different means, depending on the origin of the story, Maui was able to find this hook, and he returned to his brothers, begging to be given just one more chance. Reluctantly they agreed, and the next day he joined them in the canoes on the ocean. Then, sure enough when he lowered his line into the ocean, it immediately hooked on land. As he began to haul it up, the sea began to churn irritably and violently. Maui commanded his brothers to paddle hard, but not to turn to look. This they did, and Maui hauled on the line so the tips of mountains began to emerge from the angry sea. Urging his brothers to paddle hard and keep their eyes forward, Maui drew more peaks out of the ocean, until, defeated by curiosity, one brother glanced back and the spell was broken. Maui's line broke, and the hook was lost. It is for this reason, they say, that Hawaii is a land of incomplete mountains, each separated by the ocean.

The mountains of Hawaii, however, remained only mountains until Pele brought fire to their tips. Pele is the Hawaiian goddess of volcanoes and fire. She was born of the female spirit Haumea, a descendant of the earth goddess Papa. To Hawaii she sailed from Tahiti in a canoe guided by her brother, the shark god Ka-moho-ali'i. In the distance, she perceived the high mountain with its cloudy top, and she called the place Hawai'i. Carrying her magic stick named Pa'oa, she climbed the mountain, and finding a place where some of the earth had collapsed into a crater, she planted the stick, and before long a volcano began to spill. She called this place Kilauea, and the crater Halema'uma'u, and there she made her home. A nearby cliff was declared sacred to Ka-moho-ali'i, and to this day, neither lava or volcanic steam is allowed to touch that cliff.

In the French Polynesian Islands of Tuamotu, the story is told of Maui and his challenge to the eel-god Tuna for the sake of Hina, and his attempt to conquer death.

Hina and Tuna lived together under the sea as husband and wife. One day, however, growing tired of her life in the watery world and with the cold and inhuman god of eels, she returned to the land in search of a human husband. Passing from one village to another, she found only men who urged her to continue on her way, for they feared that Tuna would find them if they took her, and kill them. Then, as she began to despair, she happened to pass alongside the home of Huahega, and she repeated her call. Huahega heard, and instructed her last-born son, Maui tikitiki a Ataraga, to take the woman as his wife. Maui did as he was told, and the three lived happily at that place.

Soon enough the news reached Tuna that Hina was married and living with her new husband Maui at the home of his mother Huahega. For a while, he seemed not to care, but his people taunted him, for Tuna was the acme of potency, and how can he abide his queen taking her pleasure with a man of much lesser attributes, and moreover, bent at the tip. At this he grew angry and asked what sort of man was this Maui tikitiki. He is a small man, came the reply, and his *ure* is bent. At that Tuna retorted that all that would be required would be for him to show the upstart the dirty cloth between his legs, and the fool would soon enough take to his heels. Thus, Tuna began to prepare himself to take back his wife.

Word, of course, soon enough reached Maui that Tuna was preparing to deal with him, to which Maui quite rightly scoffed, but also discreetly ask what kind of "ure" is this thing Tuna.

Oh, he was told, he is enormous, bigger than a whale's, like a standing palm tree. Well, Maui replied, let him just see the crooked end of mine, and he will run for his life.

The days passed, and the sky grew darker and clouds tumbled in, and people knew that Tuna was near. The thunder rolled and the lightning crashed, and the people blamed Maui who had stolen a god's woman. Maui, however, was undismayed as Tuna arrived, riding a great wave, his loincloth stripped and his size revealed.

Then Huahega called to Maui, "Quick! Show him yours...pull it out!"

And Maui did. The wave fell back and the seabed was naked. The monsters of the deep lay floundering and helpless as Maui walked among them, killing each in turn with his weapon – all except Tuna.

It was agreed between them that they would fight, and the one who survived would have the woman. The means of combat was also decided. First Tuna would enter the body of Maui through the entrance to the rear, and in this way kill him. If he failed, it would be Maui's turn. Tuna entered Maui's body by that means, by the entrance to the rear, but after a while, when he returned, Maui was unscathed. It was then Maui's turn, and once he disappeared into the body of Tuna, the sinews of the eel god dissolved, his body fell apart, and he died.

Then, following a familiar theme, the head of Tuna was planted beside a post in the corner of Maui's house, from which, in due course, grew a plantation of coconut trees. On the nuts produced by those trees, the face of Tuna is, once again, clearly visible.

Thus Maui, Huahega and Hina lived peacefully in that house. One night, however, as Huahega slept, Maui noticed a few strands of grey in her hair. The next morning he asked her how this was so, to which she replied that it was simply a sign of her growing old and that one day soon she would die, and be buried, and be seen no more.

He asked her, "How can people live forever in the world?"

To this Huahega replied that only by acquiring and swallowing the guts of Rori-tau the Sea-slug-of-the-deep-set-eyes could achieve this.

Maui searched around the pools and lagoons for Rori, finding him eventually in the coral beds of Whangape. Knowing Maui to be a trickster, Rori was wary, and he asked the young demi-god what his purpose was. He replied, "I have come to take your stomach, in exchange for which I will give you mine."

When Rori asked if he would die by yielding his stomach, Maui tartly responded, "You will surely die if you do not." Rori would hear none of it. At that Maui seized him, and squeezed out his guts, and after vomiting out his own, he set about swallowing the stomach of Rory-tau. At that moment, however, his brothers, who had followed him to see what he was about, ran up to him, laughing and jeering that Maui was swallowing the stomach of that demon sea slug. Maui vomited, and the entrails of the sea slug landed at his feet. The opportunity was lost, and hence it is that people age, turn grey and die.

Soon afterwards Hina bore Maui two daughters, the first they named Rori-i-tau and the second Te-Aahine-hui-rori. No sons were born to the couple, and the daughters were named after Rori-tau in order that they never die.

From Tahiti comes the chilling story of Rona-nihoniho-roroa, or Rona-long-teeth, a fearsome, man-eating woman. Rona was of noble rank, and was handsome, and much admired, but because of those teeth, and what she used them for, her husband left her after the delivery of their firstborn, never to return.

The child was a daughter she named Hina. Rona loved her daughter, and cared for her well, washing her well and softening her skin every day with the oil of an aromatic sandalwood tree. She fed her only the flesh of the tenderest crabs which she caught herself on the reef at low tide. The girl grew healthy and beautiful, never knowing what food it was that her mother ate. During the day, Rona hid in a secret cave alongside a well-used footpath, and from there she caught men as they passed, and ate them.

There was one man who was not caught, however, and his name was Monoihere. Monoihere was young and handsome, and he desired Rona's daughter Hina, and she him. The two met every day in a secret place when Rona was away gathering crabs on the reef. To feed her lover, Hina always took along a small basket of crab meat. After a time, Rona began to notice that the food she spent her day gathering was disappearing quickly, and she was suspicious.

The next day, when she had prepared the usual amount of crab meat, she complained that she was unwell and she returned to her bed. When she was certain that her mother was asleep, Hina took some food and crept out of the house. Rona, of course, immediately threw aside the covers and followed a short distance behind. When she saw Hina and Monoihere meet, and share their custom, she felt a hunger for his flesh. The next morning she told Hina that she would not hunt crabs that day, but would do it under the moonlight that evening. Instead, however, she crept to the place where the two lovers met, and there she summoned Monoihere from his hiding place, pretending that she was Hina.

Monoihere was suspicious, for he knew the voice of his lover, and moreover, he recognized her mother, the dreaded Rona-long-teeth, the eater of men. Then, Rona rushed him, and caught him, and ate him, and when she was finished, she returned home to her daughter. As the moon came up, as she had promised, she gathered up her basket and spear and waded out onto the reef.

When sure she was alone, Hina took some food and hurried to the place, and there she found the remains of her lover, his viscera and his bones. However, she also found his heart, still beating, and with it she returned to her home. There she wrapped the heart of her lover in a soft tapa cloth before creating an effigy in her bed of coconuts, sticks and tapa cloth. She and her lover's heart then fled the house to take refuge in the house of a kindly chief, No'a-huruhuru.

When Rona returned home and called for Hina, she heard no reply. Enraged, she threatened the form lying inert under the covers that she would be eaten if she did not reply. Still there was silence, and Rona leaped upon the form in the bed and sunk her teeth into it. All she saw was the effigy, and then she knew that Hina was gone. For the rest of the day she searched the village until eventually she found her daughter in the home of No'a-huruhuru. She bore her terrible teeth as she prepared to devour her daughter.

No'a-huruhuru, when he saw this terrible thing about to happen, lifted his spear and plunged it into Rona's throat, killing her instantly. So perished Rona-nihoniho-roroa, the vahine kaitangata of Taharaa, the ancestor of Tahaki-kirikura, known also as "Tahaki of the Golden Skin."

In the home of No'a-huruhuru, Hina bore two sons, Punga and Hema, who both grew firm and strong. Both were expert surf-riders, known throughout the islands for their skill. One day, when the surf was right, the two boys took up their boards and prepared to leave. Hina asked Punga, her first-born, to pick the lice from her hair before he went, but he refused and left. For that Hina cursed his future wife, declaring that she would always be a woman of mediocre qualities. Then she turned to Hema, and asked him, and he returned his board to its place and sat down to do this for his mother. For that, she promised that his future wife would be a fine woman of quality and virtue.

Sure enough, when Punga took a wife, she proved to be a woman of poor qualities who bore him five sons who collectively amounted to nothing. Hema, however, found a wife descended from the gods, a woman by the name of Huauri. When the firstborn of their children arrived, he was auburn-haired and golden-skinned, and they named him Tahaki-kirikura.

Tahaki grew up strong, and excelled in all that he did, for his mother, descended from the Gods, imbued in him the power, wisdom and knowledge of her lineage. In a secret place, where no one else could see, she had Tahaki open his mouth, and above the crown of her head, breath in her knowledge and spirit. He grew to chiefly stature, sacred in all that he did, standing taller than any other man and when he walked, his footprints were embedded in the volcanic rock. His skin was the color of gold, and the *kura* was his, and all creatures who owned the color red did so because of him.[9]

Tahaki was a great hero, and the author of many deeds, the first of which was the cutting of the sinews of the fish. Tahiti was a fish, but it didn't move any more, for it had turned to land. For

---

[9] *Kura* is a word with many meanings, sometimes with religious or occult application although in this instance it probably refers to the *parekura*, or war bonnet of the Polynesians which were typically ornamented with red feathers.

Tahiti to remain ever stable in the world, the sinews of that fish required to be cut, but no mortal man came forward to take on the task, and no Gods were present to help. It was Tahaki who took up the great adze called Te-pa-huruni, used for the ceremony of Tinorua, god of the ocean, and with that he prepared to cut the sinews of the great fish Tahiti. It was desirable that the land might spread and the islands disperse, for the darkness to lift and the rain-bearing clouds find room to grow; for the wind to sweep among the peaks and mankind walk upon the shores.

The adze became possessed, becoming light in his hands, and he chopped, cutting the sinews of the fish.

Moai

Today, Easter Island is almost synonymous for the unique artifacts that grace its coastline and interior, particularly the nearly 900 monumental statues that are unlike anything found elsewhere across the globe. Known as "Moai" by the island inhabitants, these statues have amazed everyone who has seen them in person or in photos, and they have befuddled researchers attempting to answer important questions about them. The Moai also vary considerably, with the tallest having a height of over 70 feet and the shortest being less than 4 feet. With the average statue having a height of about 13 feet and a weight of several tons, it's unclear how or why the inhabitants constructed them, and given the manner in which they were positioned across certain parts of Easter Island, it's also unclear how the inhabitants transported the giant monoliths. On top of that, some researchers have speculated that only a third of the Moai made it to their intended destination on the island.

Of course, before these statues could be created, the people who made them needed to find their way to Easter Island's desolate location, which was quite literally in the middle of the nowhere. Then they also needed to learn how to settle there and survive. The story of Easter Island's statues is extraordinary, but the story of how people came to be there in the first place is just as incredible.

Easter Island's name is instantly recognizable today, but several centuries ago it had no name at all and was merely a lonely slice of land within a great expanse of ocean. Much of its surface formed when volcanoes thrust upward from the Earth's crust and filled the air with ash. That ash set solid, and the volcano, later to be named Ma'unga Terevaka, became extinct sometime during the Pleistocene era, which stretched between 2,588,000-11,700 years ago. Specifically dated at less than 400,000 years old, this volcano produced a lava field at Roiho sometime between 110,000-150,000 years ago.

The island formed through natural processes, thereby developing its own ecosystem isolated from human intervention, but its isolation was altered sometime between 700-1100, when the first of the Polynesian settlers arrived and decided to stay. The Polynesian people's expansion throughout the islands across the Pacific was made possible due to developments in seafaring technologies, as well as the ambition and prestige that went along with making sailing and navigation easier. Canoe builders were socially and politically powerful in their society due to the importance of their skills, and handlers were also specialists at their craft. They utilized tools such as drills, cordage, clamps, chisels and adzes to splice rough hewn logs and planks into seaworthy vessels. Of particular importance was a method of joinery that allowed the vessel to have both strength and flexibility, the two necessary attributes for a boat to survive the rigors of an ocean voyage.[10]

Oral tradition suggests the first landing at Easter Island took place at the Caleta Anakena landing point, a sandy beach with ideally sheltered conditions for both canoe landings and departures. However, radiocarbon evidence places the earliest settlements at Tahai. Attempting to determine the location and date of human arrival on the island, archaeologists Terry Hunt and Carl Lipo dated deposits from excavations at Anakena, noting, "Radiocarbon dates for the earliest stratigraphic layers at Anakena, Easter Island and analysis of previous radiocarbon dates imply that the island was colonized late, about 1200 CE. Significant ecological impacts and major cultural investments in monumental architecture and statuary thus began soon after initial settlement."[11]

The first settlers were likely to have journeyed by canoe or catamaran from either the Gambier Islands (about 1,600 miles away) or the Marquesas Islands (about 2,000 miles away). Ethnographic evidence cites the Rapa Nui language as very similar to Mangarevan, estimated as having an 80% similarity in vocabulary, suggesting a common ancestry.

---

[10] Tilburg, Jo Anne Van & Ralston, Ted. 2005. Megaliths and Mariners: Experimental Archaeology on Easter Island. In: Johnson, K (ed). 2005. *Onward and Upward! Papers in Honor of Clement W. Meighan.* Workwood Press Publishers, USA. Site accessed 11 September 2013. http://www.eisp.org/544/

[11] Hunt, Terry & Lipo, Carl. 2011. *The Statues that Walked: Unravelling the Mystery of Easter Island.* Free Press.

Panorama of Anakena beach

The activities that have since made Easter Island famous across the world began in the Rano Raraku volcanic crater on the lower slopes of Terevaka on Easter Island, sometime around 1200. The people known as the Rapa Nui had been settled on the island for about 100 years, living in a controlled environment with reliable sources of food, including sea life, domesticated chickens and crops of sweet potato. Under these conditions, the population had spread across the island and had begun to expand in number.[12] Culture was developing and flourishing on the island, and in this environment a new project was envisaged: the sculpting of large statues to be placed at strategic locations of religious importance around the island. The material for this enterprise was readily available, since the last eruption of volcano Ma'unga Terevaka in the Pleistocene era had deposited layers of consolidated volcanic ash that solidified into tuff. It was this stone, a distinctive yellow-brown volcanic tuff, that became the material from which the monolithic human figures were carved.[13]

The outer slope of Rano Raraku with several Moai, some of which remain unfinished

---

[12] Cambridge University Press. 2013. *The Polynesian Expansion across the Pacific (c. 700 – 1756)*. pp 272-278. Site accessed 11 September 2013. https://www.cambridge.edu.au/education/

[13] Bloch, Hannah. 2012. *Easter Island: The riddle of the moving statues*. National Geographic (National Geographic Society) 222 (1): 30–49.

The first of these Moai were small sculptures that varied greatly in their form and style. The smaller versions were also carved from varying raw materials, utilizing the different stone types that the island had to offer. It was only over time that the design, material type and process began to become more formalized. As it did, the size of the sculptures grew in scale, and a regulated quarry was required for the works to proceed. The chosen quarry was the Rano Raraku volcanic crater, where raw materials were available in abundance. There the quarry was carefully subdivided into different territories for each of the island's clans. The professional carvers, each one of high status in their society, formed the Moai with stone tools, carving the statues out of the volcanic rock. Once the statue had been shaped accordingly, it would be rubbed down with pumice to smooth its surface.

The designs for the Moai were based on ancestor worship within the island's society. The minimalist style of the statues was not dissimilar to other art and culture forms found throughout Polynesia. The column shaped figures are gifted with elongated heads, of much greater proportion to the body than is realistically found in human beings. Elongated noses and protruding lips are placed beneath sunken, hollow eyes. These hollow sockets were originally filled with coral, black obsidian and red scoria, used to make up a representation of the eye and its pupil. These have long since fallen from the statues, but remnants of them have been collected and reconstructed.[14] The bodies themselves show heavy torsos and bas relief arms depicting slender fingers resting either on the hips or meeting at the loincloth, known in the local language as the hami.

---

[14] Ford, Nick. 2011. *Theories behind the statues on Easter Island*. Site accessed 12 September 2012. http://www.helium.com/items/2210803-easter-island-environmnetal-collapse-cult-of-the-birdman

Moai at Ahu Tongariki

Legs are seldom depicted on the sculptures, but contrary to popular belief, the statues are full-bodied and not simply comprised of head and torso designs. The misunderstanding that the statues only represent facial features is mostly due to the prominent and conspicuous nature of the heads, but it is also due in part to the natural erosion on the island, which has resulted in many of the statues being buried up to their necks. This has given the impression to modern tourists that the head is all there is of the statues, and the Moai are often colloquially referred to as the Easter Island Heads.[15] Although the legs not a feature on most Moai, one of the statues, known as Tukuturi, is in a kneeling position.

---

[15] Bloch, Hannah. 2012. *Easter Island: The riddle of the moving statues*. National Geographic (National Geographic Society) 222 (1): 30–49.

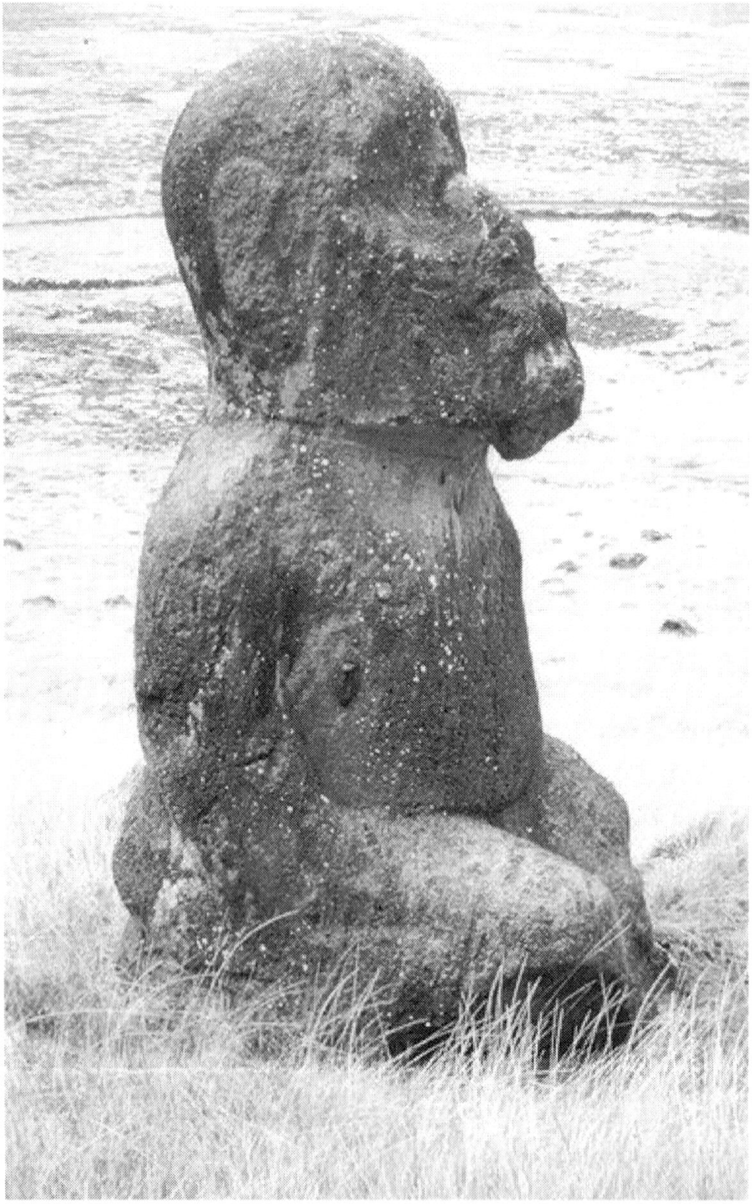

A photo of the kneeling Tukuturi taken by Brocken Inaglory

Petroglyphs were also inscribed onto the bodies of the Moai, with crescent shapes representing Polynesian canoes being a repeated motif. In her assessment of the statues and excavation of what has been interpreted as a signature stone bearing such a crescent shaped mark, UCLA archaeologist Jo Anne Van Tilburg concluded that it was likely meant to represent a carver's mark or the symbol of a family group.[16] She noted, "Over time, it seems, more of these canoes were etched onto the statue in a constant repetition of identity reasserting who they were. As the community lost a sense of identity over time, perhaps they wanted to mark these statues as their own."[17] Meanwhile, some Moai had red scoria carved pukao placed upon on their heads. Red scoria is a very light rock from a quarry at Puna Pau, and pukao were ceremonial hats or topknots. There is also evidence to suggest that the statues were originally painted red by the same red pigment that the Rapa Nui people used to coat their own bodies during times of ceremony; approximately 800 grams of natural red pigment were recovered from around the base of a Moai during archaeological excavation. The same excavation also identified human bones throughout the stratigraphic layers surrounding the statue, indicating that multiple burials took place over prolonged periods of time around the base of the statues.[18] In some instances, raw materials other than tuff were used in creating the Moai, but these were rarer. Of the 887

---

[16] Lee, Cynthia. 2012. *Archaeologist digs deep to reveal Easter Island torsos*. Site accessed 9 September 2013. http://today.ucla.edu/portal/ut/easter-island-statues-revealed-234519.aspx

[17] Lee, Cynthia. 2012. *Archaeologist digs deep to reveal Easter Island torsos*. Site accessed 9 September 2013. http://today.ucla.edu/portal/ut/easter-island-statues-revealed-234519.aspx

[18] Lee, Cynthia. 2012. *Archaeologist digs deep to reveal Easter Island torsos*. Site accessed 9 September 2013. http://today.ucla.edu/portal/ut/easter-island-statues-revealed-234519.aspx

recorded statues across Easter Island, the only non-tuff examples consist of 22 carved from trachyte, 17 carved from red scoria and 13 carved from basalt.[19]

Bjarte Sorensen's picture of a Moai at Ahu Tahai that was restored and includes the ceremonial scoria pukao hat

The average Moai is about 13 feet high, with an average width of about 5 feet. The average weight for each Moai is around 12.5 tons, making their transportation around the island just as impressive a feat as their initial manufacture in the Rano Raraku quarry. Evidence of the

---

[19] Tilburg, Jo Anne Van. 1994. *Easter Island: Archaeology, Ecology and Culture*. Washington, DC: Smithsonian Institution Press. pp 24.

technology that was used to move the Moai and to raise them upright has also been located during archaeological excavation. According to the available evidence, a deep round post hole was excavated and a shaped tree trunk was placed there in close proximity to the stone. Ropes were then attached to the trunk, guided around the statue by cuttings made in the bedrock surrounding the statue itself. The carving was completed in stages as the stone was gradually raised, with the front carved while it was upright and the back finished once the statue had been raised to a fully erect position.[20] It has been hypothesized that similar wood and rope technologies were utilized in the transport of the stone, with wooden sleds and rollers being a possibility. It's possible that these sleds and/or rollers used leveled tracks around the island.[21] The mythological stories of the Rapa Nui account for the movement of the statues by other means, recounting instances of divine power used to command the statues to walk. King Tuu Ku Ihu was one ruler who apparently moved the Moai with the help of the creator god Makemake. Another tale tells of a woman living alone on the mountain possessing the strength of will to order the statues to move.[22]

Regardless of how the transportation was accomplished, hundreds of Moai were ultimately moved from the quarry to various locations around the island, and they generally face inward from the shoreline with their backs toward the ocean (aside from a few exceptions). They were set on stone platforms called ahu, which often supported several Moai and included elaborate designs. For example, the ahu had walls around the platform, the ramps that were ostensibly used to transport and raise the statues upright, and even plazas in front of the them

Once they were erected, the Moai were apparently considered religious items. The original meanings associated with them have been lost, but it is likely that they represented the embodiment of chiefs, both living and deceased. What is known of the Moai is that they were part of ancestor worship practices on Easter Island. In that sense, they were probably lineage status symbols of great importance as well.

As the ecological pressures of increased population, diminished food resources and deforestation combined to destabilize the culture of the Rapa Nui, a change occurred in their practices. The Rano Raraku quarry appears to have been abandoned very quickly, as evidenced by what was left there. The Rapa Nui left their stone tools at the site, as well as completed Moai ready for transport and numerous unfinished statues, all left within the quarry area. While there's no doubt that was all partly the result of abandonment, researchers have since developed other theories to explain what was left in the quarry. For example, it's been suggested that some statues were intentionally left incomplete because of issues in the quality of the tuff, and others think it's possible that the finished statues were positioned there and intended to remain there

---

[20] Lee, Cynthia. 2012. *Archaeologist digs deep to reveal Easter Island torsos*. Site accessed 9 September 2013. http://today.ucla.edu/portal/ut/easter-island-statues-revealed-234519.aspx

[21] Bloch, Hannah. 2012. *Easter Island: The riddle of the moving statues*. National Geographic (National Geographic Society) 222 (1): 30–49.

[22] History Channel. 2009. *Mega Movers: Ancient Mystery Moves*. A&E Home Video, USA.

permanently. It has even been alleged that some of the statues were never meant to be finished anyway.

The abandonment of the site has been attributed to any number of multiple disasters that struck the island, including disease, food shortage, and attacks by Europeans and slave traders. Some oral histories make reference to the Earth shaking, which supposedly toppled many of the Maoi around the island, but there is also evidence that after Dutch explorer Jacob Roggeveen visited the island in 1722, he killed a number of inhabitants, which may have prompted some of the Rapa Nui to intentionally topple some of their own Moai.[23]

Mythology and Conspiracy Theories on Easter Island

When Europeans first began arriving in the 18th century, they talked to inhabitants on Easter Island, and the inhabitants relayed the history of their ancestors. According to those inhabitants, Easter Island once had a strong class system. At the time of ancestor worship and the construction of the Moai, the Rapa Nui belonged to several different clans, each of which had their own chief, but there was also an ariki (or high chief) who wielded power over all of the clans and their respective chiefs. The high chief traced his ancestry all the way back to the legendary founder of Easter Island (at least according to the Rapa Nui legends), Hotu Matu'a. The Moai that were placed around the island linked the current inhabitants with their ancestors, with burial practice undertaken around the Moai also linking the living and dead.

Around 1540, however, these concepts of power, previously attributed to hereditary leaders and symbolized through the ancestor worship of the Moai, changed, and they were subsequently vested in the figure of a mythical Bird Man. This mythical Bird Man became the medium by which the living were linked to their ancestors, rather than the statues which had previously served this role in Rapa Nui culture. The mythical god that the Rapa Nui saw as responsible for them, Makemake, also played a part in this process. The island became decorated with numerous petroglyphs during the time of the Bird Man cult, with cave interiors often utilized for this purpose.[24] The petroglyphs are very similar to ones identified in Hawaii, suggesting that the Bird Man mythology was something with commonality across the many settlers of the Polynesian islands. If the Bird Man myth was brought by the early settlers to the island however, there was one development that was truly unique to Easter Island.

---

[23] Edwards, Edmundo; Marchetti, Raul; Dominichetti, Leopoldo & Gonzales-Ferran, Oscar. 1996. "When the Earth Trembled, the Statues Fell". In: *Rapa Nui Journal* 10 (1). pp 1-15.

[24] UNESCO. 1995. *Rapa Nui National Park*. Site accessed 11 September 2013. http://whc.unesco.org/en/list/715

A petroglyph depicting the god Makemake and birdmen, carved out of red scoria

This unique tradition consisted of competitions undertaken for the Bird Man, which started sometime around 1760 but ended in 1878 after they forcibly stamped out by Roman Catholic missionaries, who built a mission on the island and set about converting its population to Christianity. The competition was highly dangerous, and many inhabitants on the island died, either by falling to their deaths, drowning, or even being eaten by sharks. The ritual was an annual one that required competitors to collect the first Sooty Tern (manu tara) egg of the season. These were collected from the rocky islet of Motu Nui, after which the competitors had to swim back from there with the egg and then climb the sea cliff of Rano Kau to the cliff-top village of Orongo. The winner of the contest was dubbed the Tangata manu (or Bird Man). There was a high level of ritual and mysticism associated with the contest as well. For example, the competitors were chosen by ivi-attuas, or prophets, who claimed to see the chosen competitors in their dreams.[25]

---

[25] Haun, Beverley. 2008. *Inventing 'Easter Island'*. University of Toronto Press. pp 8.

Picture of Motu Nui by Ian Sewell

The location of Orongo, with petroglyphs in the rock. Photo by Rivi

A final task was still required after the egg's collection. Contestants that had been unsuccessful had to return to Orongo, while the winner remained in Motu Nui. The winner, the ritualized Bird Man, would remain there until he was spiritually prepared to return. Upon returning, he presented his egg to his patron, who would have shaved his head in preparation and painted it either white or red.

The Tangata-Manu, with egg in hand, then led a procession down the hill to either Rano Raraku (if he was from the eastern clans) or to Anakena (if he was from the western clans). Either way, once he returned to his clan, he was considered to be tapu (or sacred) for a period of five months, and during this time, he would wear a headdress made from human hair and let his nails grow. He would be given a new name, gifted with food and other tributes, and spend the next year in seclusion in a special ceremonial house.

The Tangata-Manu wasn't the only one to benefit from winning the contest; his entire clan was awarded sole rights to collect the next season's harvest of fledglings and wild bird eggs from the rocky islet of Motu Nui as well.[26] It is ironic that the egg hunt, a part of contemporary Easter traditions in the Western world, was present in this dangerous form at a place called Easter Island. The egg hunting tradition of Easter celebrations derives from Babylonian myths, pagan rituals of spring rebirth, and the fertility lore of the Indo-European races, all transposed much later onto Christian stories and incorporated into the Passover holy day as it transformed in the Christian traditions of the modern world.[27] The reality of an unrelated egg hunt ritualized in the traditional customs of Easter Island surely demonstrates that the truth can be stranger than fiction.

In addition to cave areas, petroglyphs and the Moai, the Easter Island area also has archaeological value in the remnants of the Orongo ceremonial village. This village area was once the Bird Man religious center and part of a complex of religious practices enacted by the people of Easter Island during the period of the Bird Man worship. The extant village today includes more than 50 semi-subterranean stone houses. These houses were built in contiguous groups, positioned together along the rim of the Ran Kay crater under the overshadowing presence of a towering cliff face. These stone houses were called hare, and the island also contains remnants of earlier houses constructed by inhabitants of the island from periods of time prior to the Bird Man cult era.

When originally built, the houses were raised onto basalt foundations, and other associated structures were built in proximity as well, such as hearths, farm buildings, ovens and even chicken houses made from stone. Round stone towers were also built into some houses, usually on those that were located close to the coast. The remnants of the Orongo ceremonial village are the most complete on the island, and they provide insight into how the people of Easter Island lived their lives and interacted with others in their society.[28]

---

[26] Gosford, Bob. 2009. *El Ritual del Hombre-Pajaro – the bird-man cult of Rapa Nui*. Site accessed 12 September 2013. http://blogs.crikey.com.au/northern/2009/05/19/el-ritual-del-hombre-pajaro-the-bird-man-cult-of-rapa-nui/
[27] Pack, David C. 2013. *The True Origin of Easter*. Site accessed 12 September 2013. http://rcg.org/books/ttooe.html
[28] UNESCO. 1995. *Rapa Nui National Park*. Site accessed 11 September 2013. http://whc.unesco.org/en/list/715

Restored stone houses at Orongo

In 1995, UNESCO designated Easter Island a World Heritage Site, ensuring that much of the island is now protected as part of Rapa Nui National Park. One of only 981 properties protected worldwide for their unique natural and cultural heritage values, the listing states, "Rapa Nui, the indigenous name of Easter Island, bears witness to a unique cultural phenomenon. A society of Polynesian origin that settled there c. A.D. 300 established a powerful, imaginative and original tradition of monumental sculpture and architecture, free from any external influence. From the 10th to the 16th century this society built shrines and erected enormous stone figures known as Moai , which created an unrivalled cultural landscape that continues to fascinate people throughout the world." In addition to the Moai, cave dwellings, stone houses, rock art and engravings are also cited as essential parts of the importance of the location.[29]

The UNESCO listing has certainly boosted the continuing tourist trade, which has built up ever since the first refueling flights began to stop on the island. In 2007, a vote was taken to name Easter Island one of the new seven wonders of the world. Although Easter Island made the top ten selections, it was not one of the seven chosen. Nevertheless, one of the island's residents, an ex-Chilean turned Easter Island scuba diver, mentioned just how strong the existing tourist industry already was by that time: "We have more than 50,000 visitors during the year, which means more than 11 times the total population of the island." He added, "[W]e would prefer a

---

[29] UNESCO. 1995. *Rapa Nui National Park*. Site accessed 11 September 2013. http://whc.unesco.org/en/list/715

high-quality tourism. Maybe not more people, but people with more money asking for more professional services."

Of course, the preservation of the Moai and other archaeological treasures across Easter Island, a place now thought of by many as one large open air museum, is integral to the long term survival of the ever growing tourism industry. With some monuments eroding due to natural forces and other sites damaged through mistreatment or neglect, the attempt to be named one of the new wonders of the world also brought attention to the island's plight. As one writer noted, "[W]hen Rapa Nui became one of the candidates to be one of wonders of the world, it was also an (alarm) bell for the authorities to say wake up and look at what's going on around. If we haven't learned anything from the past -- the good and the bad -- then we're blind." [30]

Another part of the international attraction to the island has come from the mythology that has sprung up over its unique statues and their entry as icons into worldwide popular culture. This is due at least in part to fringe theorist Erich von Daniken's descriptions of the Moai in his book *Chariots of the Gods*. In his book, von Daniken argued that the native inhabitants could not have made the Moai, asserting that "whole mountain massifs had been transformed, steel-hard volcanic rock had been cut through like butter and 10,000 tons of massive rocks lay in places where they could not have been dressed." He also pointed out that since "no trees grow on the island… the usual explanation, that the stone giants were moved to their present sites on wooden rollers, is not feasible." He then suggested that the answer may lie in one interpretation of the island's name – "Land of the bird men" - with the statues appearing "like robots which seem to be waiting solely to be set in motion again," perhaps by the creatures of legend he states may once have really been there, the aliens who von Daniken argues were the true architects for these sculptures. "The legend is confirmed," he concludes, "by sculptures of flying creatures with big staring eyes."[31]

Von Daniken's central argument about the achievements of the past is that humans did not have the capacity to attain such successes and were therefore not responsible for the great monuments of antiquity. His book instead suggests a utopian past when space travelers, possibly native Martians seeking to escape changing environmental condition on their own world, escaped to Earth and brought a wealth of knowledge and technology along with them.[32] As he describes it, "[A] group of Martian giants perhaps escaped to Earth to found the new culture of homo sapiens by breeding with the semi-intelligent beings living there… giants who come from the stars, who could move enormous blocks of stone, who instructed men in arts still unknown on Earth and who finally died out."[33]

---

[30] Ross, Jen. 2010. *Easter Island still attracts more tourists than it can handle*. Site accessed 13 September 2013. http://www.canada.com/travel/Easter+Island+still+attracts+more+tourists+than+handle/920477/story.html
[31] von Daniken, Erich. 1972. *Chariots of the Gods? Was God an Astronaut?* Gorgi, Great Britain. pp 113-115.
[32] von Daniken, Erich. 1972. *Chariots of the Gods? Was God an Astronaut?* Gorgi, Great Britain. pp 99.
[33] von Daniken, Erich. 1972. *Chariots of the Gods? Was God an Astronaut?* Gorgi, Great Britain. pp 155.

Of course, von Daniken's evidence is based upon the island's lack of material, and it rests on the argument that without wooden rollers, the monumental statues could not have been moved, and that since the island is deforested, there would have been no material in the past to provide such rollers. The basic error made by von Daniken is a recurring one; modern viewers assume the world of the past looked the same as it does in the present. To the contrary, when humans first arrived on Easter Island, it was densely forested; in fact, it was precisely the humans' overuse of the available resources that brought about the ecological changes von Daniken discussed in the book. Today's inhabitants on Easter Island would be ill-equipped to produce monumental statues based on the resources available now, but the Rapa Nui of the past had everything they required.

Von Daniken's theory devalued the ingenuity of human ability; after all, the Polynesian settlers had mixed great ambition with impressive technological accomplishments just to reach Easter Island in the first place. However, von Daniken's argument still strikes a chord with pop culture and New Age beliefs, and the linking of the Easter Island heads with aliens and the paranormal has become a part of the popular culture iconography in the modern world. The Moai design has appeared everywhere from t-shirts to magazine covers and computer games. In 2011, an exhibition was held at the Kon-Tiki Museum on Easter Island to celebrate these links, and the exhibition was titled "Island, Myths and Popular Culture". The exhibition was designed to explore the various ways in which "Easter Island has been popularized in fiction, and in material and visual culture". In addition to the exhibition itself, a website was set up with educational support provided both for schools and researchers who might be "wishing to gain a view on Easter Island through an understanding of the power and the extent of the myths that, in particular, circulate around the Moai". One of the many striking images includes a magazine cover illustration where an alien space man stands beside the rock carving of an ancient Moai. Clad in a space suit resplendent with fish bowl style globe helmet, the face of this alien space man exactly matches that of the Moai he stands beside. Such images have nothing to do with historical reality, but they certainly do provide some pop culture fun and also help generate interest in the Moai and Easter Island.[34]

Regardless of the different associations, the reality is that the Moai, such potent symbols of the past, are just as prevalent in today's global culture as they were within the isolated society of Rapa Nui's past. They continue to inspire the thoughts and imaginations of people from across the globe, ranging from tourists to academics and everyone in between, ensuring that the first explorers of the Polynesian islands who set out to conquer the great unknown of the Pacific Ocean over a thousand years ago ultimately left a legacy that will continue to flourish long into the future.

---

[34] Moai Culture. 2011. Easter Island Myths and Popular Culture. Site accessed 11 September 2013. http://www.Moaiculture.appspot.com/

Online Resources

Other titles about Polynesia on Amazon

Bibliography

Alibaba. 2013. Big Moai Products. Site accessed 12 September 2013. http://www.alibaba.com/showroom/big-Moai.html

Belich, James, Making Peoples: A History of the New Zealanders from the Polynesian settlement to the end of the 19th century (1996)

Belich, James, Paradise Reforged: A History of the New Zealanders from 1880 to the Year 2000 (2001).

Bloch, Hannah. 2012. Easter Island: The riddle of the moving statues. National Geographic (National Geographic Society) 222 (1): 30–49.

Byrnes, Giselle (2009). The New Oxford History of New Zealand. Oxford University Press.

Cambridge University Press. 2013. The Polynesian Expansion across the Pacific (c. 700 – 1756). pp 275. Site accessed 11 September 2013. https://www.cambridge.edu.au/education/

Cook, James. 1774. The Journal of Captain Cook. March 1774 - (off Easter Island). Site accessed 11 September 2013. http://www.captaincooksociety.com/Home/Detail/tabid/126/ArticleId/929/March-1774-off-Easter-Island.aspx

Darwin, Charles. 1859. On the Origin of Species by Means of Natural Selection, or the Preservation of Favoured Races in the Struggle for Life. John Murray, London.

Ebay.com. 2013. MOAI STONE HEAD PLUSH 230 cc FW or UT HEADCOVER JAPAN. Site accessed 12 September 2013. http://www.ebay.com.au/itm/MOAI-STONE-HEAD-PLUSH-230-cc-FW-UT-HEADCOVER-JAPAN-/110799302514#vi-content

Edwards, Edmundo; Marchetti, Raul; Dominichetti, Leopoldo & Gonzales-Ferran, Oscar. 1996. "When the Earth Trembled, the Statues Fell". In: Rapa Nui Journal 10 (1). pp 1-15.

Flenley, John R. & Bahn, Paul G. 2003. The Enigmas of Easter Island. Oxford University Press, UK.

Ford, Nick. 2011. Theories behind the statues on Easter Island. Site accessed 12 September 2012. http://www.helium.com/items/2210803-easter-island-environmnetal-collapse-cult-of-the-birdman

Garman, Samuel. 1917. "The Galapagos tortoises". Memoirs of the Museum of Comparative Zoology at Harvard College 30 (4).

Gosford, Bob. 2009. El Ritual del Hombre-Pajaro – the bird-man cult of Rapa Nui. Site accessed 12 September 2013. http://blogs.crikey.com.au/northern/2009/05/19/el-ritual-del-hombre-pajaro-the-bird-man-cult-of-rapa-nui/

Haase, Karsten M; Stoffers, Peter & Garbe-Schönberg, C. Dieter. 1997. The Petrogenetic Evolution of Lavas from Easter Island and Neighbouring Seamounts, Near-ridge Hotspot Volcanoes in the SE Pacific. In: Oxford Journals. 1997. Journal of Petrology 38 (06): 785–813. Site accessed 11 September 2013. http://petrology.oxfordjournals.org

Haun, Beverley. 2008. Inventing 'Easter Island'. University of Toronto Press.

Heyerdahl, Thor. 1989. Easter Island: The Mystery Solved. Random House.

History Channel. 2009. Mega Movers: Ancient Mystery Moves. A&E Home Video, USA.

Hunt, Terry & Lipo, Carl. 2011. The Statues that Walked: Unravelling the Mystery of Easter Island. Free Press.

King, Michael (2003) The Penguin History of New Zealand.

La Estrella. 2002. Primeros datos del Censo: Hay 37.626 mujeres más que hombres en la V Región. Site accessed 11 September 2013. http://www.estrellavalpo.cl/site/edic/20020611093623/pags/20020611124031.html

Lee, Cynthia. 2012. Archaeologist digs deep to reveal Easter Island torsos. Site accessed 9 September 2013. http://today.ucla.edu/portal/ut/easter-island-statues-revealed-234519.aspx

Moai Culture. 2011. Easter Island Myths and Popular Culture. Site accessed 11 September 2013. http://www.Moaiculture.appspot.com/

New World Encyclopedia. 2013. New World Encyclopedia: Easter Island. Site accessed 11 September 2013. http://www.newworldencyclopedia.org/entry/Easter_Island

Pack, David C. 2013. The True Origin of Easter. Site accessed 12 September 2013. http://rcg.org/books/ttooe.html

Polynesian Voyaging Society. 2012. Hawaiian Voyaging Traditions. The Voyage to Rapa Nui 1999–2000. Site accessed 11 September 2013. http://pvs.kcc.hawaii.edu/

Reynolds, Kevin & Costner, Kevin (directors). 1994. Rapa Nui. Majestic Films International, USA. Site accessed 11 September 2013. http://www.imdb.com/title/tt0110944/

Ross, Jen. 2010. Easter Island still attracts more tourists than it can handle. Site accessed 13 September 2013.

Rothstein, Bo. 2005. Social traps and the problem of trust. Cambridge University Press.

Sharpe, Andrew. 1963. Ancient Voyagers in Polynesia. Longman Paul Ltd.

Sharpe, Andrew (ed). 1970. The Journal of Jacob Roggeveen. Oxford University Press.

Tilburg, Jo Anne Van. 1994. Easter Island: Archaeology, Ecology and Culture. Washington, DC. Smithsonian Institution Press.

Tilburg, Jo Anne Van & Ralston, Ted. 2005. Megaliths and Mariners: Experimental Archaeology on Easter Island. In: Johnson, K (ed). 2005. Onward and Upward! Papers in Honor of Clement W. Meighan. Workwood Press Publishers, USA. Site accessed 11 September 2013. http://www.eisp.org/544/

Todos los derechos reservados. 2013. Portal Rapa Nui. Site accessed 11 September 2013. http://www.portalrapanui.cl/

UNESCO. 1995. Rapa Nui National Park. Site accessed 11 September 2013. http://whc.unesco.org/en/list/715

von Daniken, Erich. 1972. Chariots of the Gods? Was God an Astronaut? Gorgi, Great Britain.

Leveridge, Steven. "Another Great War? New Zealand interpretations of the First World War towards and into the Second World War" First World War Studies (2016) 7#3:303-25.

Free Books by Charles River Editors

We have brand new titles available for free most days of the week. To see which of our titles are currently free, click on this link.

Discounted Books by Charles River Editors

We have titles at a discount price of just 99 cents everyday. To see which of our titles are currently 99 cents, click on this link.

Printed in Great Britain
by Amazon